T0374309

ANATHEMA

Volume XVIII

BY: TODD ANDREW ROHRER

iUniverse, Inc.
New York   Bloomington

Anathema
Volume XVIII

iUniverse books may be ordered through booksellers or by contacting:

iUniverse
1663 Liberty Drive
Bloomington, IN 47403
www.iuniverse.com
1-800-Authors (1-800-288-4677)

ISBN: 978-1-4502-4101-4 (pbk)
ISBN: 978-1-4502-4102-1 (ebk)

Printed in the United States of America

iUniverse rev. date: 7/7/10

4/28/2010 4:28:39 AM –

Mankind invented written language and math roughly five thousand years ago. In learning those inventions mankind fundamentally changed his perception not because of the inventions solely but because the inventions favored the left hemisphere of the brain so much anyone that learned those inventions altered their mental perception because in order to continue to use said inventions one had to continually favor left hemisphere. One had to favor their left hemisphere to such an extreme to master and remain proficient with said inventions a being inadvertently alters their perception to a devastating degree. The perception altering was subtle and at the same time devastating because it was taught to beings starting at a young age and in some cases twenty years before their cognitive ability which is relative to the frontal lobe even matured. Some of the most obvious side effects of this perception altering are fear or timidity and a profound awareness of time. Mankind in learning these inventions turned itself from a fearless being into a fearful timid being. Mankind became timid about pictures, sounds, words, colors and ideas and so this fear caused mankind to not be able to think clearly and so mankind's cognitive ability was hindered. Mankind started making decisions based on timidity and fear and also numbers instead of awareness and understanding and that is how mankind will perhaps remain.

"A creative man is motivated by the desire to achieve, not by the desire to beat others." - Ayn Rand

Creativity encourages experimentation not competition. Achieving further understandings does not require exploiting others.

Creativity: the ability to use the imagination to develop new and original ideas or things, especially in an artistic context.

Imagination: the ability to form images and ideas in the mind, especially of things never seen or experienced directly.

Intuition: something known or believed instinctively, without actual evidence for it; the state of being aware of or knowing something without having to discover or perceive it, or the ability to do this.

Firstly, creativity is a right brain trait but it is actually an aspect that is achieved as a result of other primary right brain traits. Creativity is relative to intuition, ambiguity, and complexity which are all right brain traits. Ambiguity allows one to achieve this free spirit or open-mindedness and that is paramount to creativity. This means a closed mind, one that has ambiguity veiled, is detrimental to creativity. The ambiguity aspect is what allows one to "eat crow" in order to improve or in order to progress in understandings. As ambiguity decreases potential intelligence decreases. If one cannot look at what they have on their plate and judge it or doubt its quality they may be trapped with improper food forever. This is relative to the concept that suggests belief hinders intelligence. As knowing increases intelligence decreases but this is not an absolute and is a symptom the actual language has many flaws because words tend to be based on absolutes.

"Philosophy is the highest music." –Plato

Philosophy is simply doubting or questioning things or ideals or concepts and this means one has to have the ambiguity aspect of right brain factoring into their conscious perception in order to achieve this mental state of questioning fully. This may appear to be a person that questions everything but in reality it is a questioning attitude about what is. Questioning something does not mean ones does not believe it, it is just a method of keeping the mind processing. The ambiguity allows one to consider every possible solution or angle and then question every angle and this creates this intelligence gaining aspect. One's ability to question things is relative to their intelligence. When the species has figured everything out about everything we can stop asking questions is another way to look at it, and until then we question everything and question why we question everything because we do not know where a question may lead relative to achieving further intelligence. As questions diminish the closed mind aspect increases. A small child will ask many questions to the point a scribe parent may just yell out "Stop asking so many questions.", and so it is clear who the closed minded one is. A tyranny relies on the slaves not asking questions. In a tyranny creative people are frowned upon and this is relative to the comment "a starving artist." In a tyranny the less one thinks the fewer questions they ask and they in turn make fantastic slaves because when one stops asking questions their intelligence diminishes. This is why it important to have right hemisphere traits, namely ambiguity, at full power at all times.

[A creative man is motivated by the desire to achieve] Sometimes in an authority meeting an authority figure will say "I don't have time for any more questions." That's a nice way of saying "I have run out of answers so I wonder why you even elected me as an authority to begin with." All questions factually lead to an understanding now matter what and so the question is not always as important as the answer. Suggesting a good question is suggesting judgment of the question but all questions are only leading one to come up with another question so the quality of the question is not as important as the questioning itself. One might ask "Why is this oil slick on the ocean threatening the estuary?" and an authority may suggest "Because the oil rig in the ocean blew up and is now leaking oil creating the oil slick that is threatening the estuary." Then one may ask "Why would you build an oil rig in the ocean that may blow up and threaten the estuary?" and the answer may be "Because we voted to build that oil rig in the ocean that may blow up and threaten the estuary." Then one may ask "Why would we vote to threaten the estuary with an oil slick" And the answer may be "Because we do not have very good cognitive ability or foresight." Then one may ask "Why do we not have very good cognitive ability or foresight?" and one may answer "Because the written education we forced by law on everyone with the compulsory education laws favors left brain traits and thus veils right brain traits and thus creates beings with poor cognitive ability because intuition is relative to cognitive ability and that is a right brain trait so it is logical a being with cognition problems would vote in favor of drilling an oil rig in the ocean that may explode and destroy the estuary and thus the beings vote to hang their self because they rely on that estuary." So then one may ask "So we have an oil slick that is threatening the estuary because we voted to have an oil rig that could blow up and that is because we voted to force education by law on ourselves and that hindered our cognitive ability because we voted and made it a law to hinder our cognitive ability knowingly or unknowingly with the

4

education technology?" And the answer may be "Yes we bring all of these problems on ourselves because we keep voting to hinder our cognitive ability and then do not apply the remedy to that problem created by the education technology and that is relative to a lack of cognitive ability or foresight." Then one may ask "Why?" And one may answer "Because we are insane from all that left brain favoring education and are no longer able to make reasonable decisions as a collective species because we never apply the remedy to the mental hindering caused by the education technology because we are too mentally hindered to even determine what the remedy is and unable to determine if it is even required because we cannot reason while mentally hindered."

The problem with asking questions is one is limited to the intelligence of the being they are asking questions to. One is not going to get very far asking questions to a tyrant. One is not going to get very far asking questions to a conditioned closed minded wall. Ambiguity is relative to perception or how one senses things, including how one sees ideas and concepts.

Intelligence: the ability to learn facts and skills and apply them, especially when this ability is highly developed.

How does one [learn facts and skills]? By experimenting and questioning. Traditional education frowns on questions. Teachers say "Go read this chapter and do the homework." Traditional education is in fact telling a person what to think and not allowing a person to determine what they wish to think. "You spell the word cat "cat" or you fail." That is not encouraging the ability to learn facts and skills. Learning is not having concepts crammed down your throat it is accomplished by questioning what the facts are. This of course is not an absolute and very few things are absolutes they are simply probabilities. It is probable if you stop questioning things you have ceased improving your intelligence and intelligence is relative to making mistakes and thinking about those mistakes as required aspects to increase intelligence so the mistakes are not really mistakes. If one cannot "eat crow", make mistakes, then ones intelligence suffers. Ability to "eat crow" is relative to pride and ego and thus pride and ego is relative to intelligence. The less pride and ego one has the more probable it is they have intelligence. This means a person with very a strong pride and ego is probably quite stupid.

Stupid: regarded as showing a lack of intelligence, perception, or common sense.

A person may say "I take pride in my country" and that is simply saying they are perhaps quite stupid because they should question their country in order to make it more intelligent or encourage it to progress in intelligence. "I take pride in my work." That means their work probably sucks because they are more concerned with being "perfect" than with becoming intelligent. One cannot be perfect and make mistakes at the same time so as mistakes decrease intelligence decreases and chance of perfection increases and thus perfection is a symptom of stupidity or lack of intelligence. All of society is based on the premise "We are not pleased with mistakes." and so all of society is probably stupid.

So there is the oil rig leaking oil and threatening the estuary and the estuary is relative to the environment and nothing can live if the environment dies, so one has to consider this aspect of intelligence: [facts and skills and apply them]. Is it the first time an oil slick has ever happened and ruined an estuary? No. So we are repeating the same mistakes over and over. We are coming to understandings but we are not applying the facts learned so we are not very intelligent. Oil is important for money but if the oil destroys the environment then we die and so the money is no longer important and thus the oil although it is worth money is meaningless because it is probable it will destroy the environment and so the environment trump's oil and money. This is elementary intelligence but that is not relevant and that is not the core problem, it is a symptom of the core problem. A colony of ant's is perhaps more intelligent than the human species relative to deeds and actions so something is out of harmony. A colony of ants does not destroy their environment relative to making the environment inhospitable for them to live in but human beings do, so the ants are in fact more intelligent than the human species and the question is, why?

X = a creature that destroys its environment so that the environment is no longer viable.

Y = a creature that does not destroy the environment so the environment remains viable.

Z = probability of survival

A = Intelligence

X + A = Z

Y + A = Z

If a creature destroys the system it relies on to survive then the creature has become suicidal and that is relative to intelligence, the mind, and psychology.

Harmony: a situation in which there is friendly agreement or accord.

So the oil slick is in the ocean and nearing the estuary and perhaps no human being will die from that but perhaps many other life forms will die and so one species is doing something that is killing other species. So the species in that estuary are perhaps in harmony with their environment but that is not relevant because there is another spices that is out of harmony and the species in that estuary are at their mercy. The earth could have a million viable species and one mentally nonviable species and that one mentally nonviable species can kill off all the mentally viable species. This is relative to the concept that a chain is only as strong as its weakest link. Disharmony seeks disharmony and spreads disharmony by its very nature.

Disharmony: lack of balance in something such as the body or the environment.

If human beings were in mental harmony they would not determine to build an oil rig on the ocean because they would have the cognitive ability to understand it is possible that rig may leak oil into the ocean creating an oil slick and thus threaten the environment they live in and thus threaten their survival and thus harm their self, probably. A human being that is insane or not capable of cognitive ability would come up with an argument relative to disharmony. "We make money off of oil so it is okay if we destroy the environment because the environment is secondary to money and thus oil." That argument is a symptom that the beings cognitive ability is no longer viable meaning one can no longer make decisions relative to harmony but relative to their perception they are making harmonious decisions which are in fact disharmonious. Disharmony perceives disharmony is harmony and so disharmony would tend to see harmony as disharmony.

If the human species was in mental harmony we would tend to never do anything that would permanently ruin the environment relative to the environment no longer being able to support life. The issue about the environment is secondary to what has caused us to be out of harmony. We are killing off other species and in the process we are killing off our self and this aspect is not probable if we are mentally in harmony relative to cognitive ability so it can only be we are mentally unbalanced as a species relative to cognitive ability. The oil slick is proof as a species we are making cognitive decisions relative to mental disharmony. If the entire species was not interested in oil we would not be drilling for it in the ocean so the reason we are drilling for it in the ocean is because of contact or peer pressure from the species so the disharmony is relative to the entire species. Our species is not a closed set. There is no such thing as countries or separate human being species separated by borders. Our base genetics do not change from border to border. One country drills in the ocean for oil and all countries do, so the country aspect is just an illusion. Human beings are determining it is wise to drill for oil in the ocean even though it is possible the oil rig may blow up and leak oil into the ocean and destroy estuary systems so that is relative to symptoms the species is not making proper cognitive decisions because the estuary is relative to the human species survival. Relative to the human species the only relevant question in the universe is: What has made us stupid? All other questions are leading to that one question. All other symptoms are leading to that one question. All understandings lead to that one question: What has made us as a species stupid?

Stupid: regarded as showing a lack of intelligence, perception, or common sense.

Something factually made our species stupid because there are oil rigs in the ocean that can blow up and leak oil into the ocean and destroy estuary systems so we cannot be anything but stupid, so what made us stupid? If you do not think as a species we are stupid it is only because you perhaps are stupid.

Voyeur: a fascinated observer of distressing, sordid, or scandalous events.

If one assumes victory is possible, then they may start to assume victory is probable, then failure will be probable.

4/30/2010 4:52:59 AM -

 "Contradictions do not exist. Whenever you think you are facing a contradiction, check your premises. You will find that one of them is wrong."- Ayn Rand

This is saying in spirit, paradox is often mistaken for contradiction and complexity is relative to paradox. There are many labels and labels cause problems because all that left brain education causes one to see way too many parts, seeing parts is a left brain trait. The education is thought control because one is born and they do not see as many parts and even after a few years of the education they start seeing lots of parts.

One can look at education as a drug that makes one see too many parts.

[Contradictions do not exist]

Contradiction: something that has aspects that are illogical or inconsistent with each other.

Illogical: apparently unreasonable or perverse, especially in not being or not giving the expected response.

Paradox: a statement, proposition, or situation that seems to be absurd or contradictory, but in fact is or may be true.

[You are good. You are bad.] The labels "good" and "bad" are relative so one cannot really make that statement in a logical fashion. It is illogical you are capable of being good or bad on an absolute level but it is possible you are capable of being good and bad at the exact same time. Anyone who says they are good or they are bad is not very logical because those labels do not really exist.

Label: a word or phrase used to describe a person or group.

Society loves the label: "That person needs help." That person probably needs help getting away from the scribes but perhaps does not need help from the scribes. Usually when a being has run out of ideas they start throwing around labels. Complexity tends to negate labels and thus contradictions. For example: [Written education is good. Written education is bad.] One has to have these right brain aspects called complexity and paradox at full power to understand that comment is not a contradiction it is a paradox.

X = written education and math

Y = good

Z = bad

A = circumstances in which written education is taught.

X + A = Y

X + A = Z

Both of these comments are valid and logical at the exact same time so it is not a contradiction it is a paradox. There are infinite ways to describe good and bad and eventually the word "bad" is going to come up in the explanation of good and eventually the word "good" is going to come up in the explanation of bad. If one thinks written education is good in an absolute way that only demonstrates they are simple minded because they got far too much of that left brain education and left brain only deals with linear simple minded aspects contrary to right brains complexity and paradox traits. The problem with the education is it forces one to think in simple minded absolutes and thus one tends to disfavor complexity.

5/1/2010 12:17:30 PM –

Time: a dimension that enables two identical events occurring at the same point in space to be distinguished, measured by the interval between the events.

The word "I" is Latin for EGO. The word "Me" denotes "I" and also denotes ego.

The word "time" has "I" and "me" in it.

A being that gets all that left brain favoring education and does not apply the remedy has what you know as strong pride or ego and a side effect of that is a strong sense of time which means a strong sense of "I" and "me" which is ego or pride. Fear is also a symptom of ego and thus no fear denotes no ego and no ego denotes no sense of time perception. As fear decreases so does ego and so does sense of time.

[Time: a dimension] denotes "No time" is also a dimension because without one dimension a contrary perception dimension is perhaps not possible. There cannot be a time dimension and then no "no sense of time" perception dimension, perhaps. Time dimension denotes awareness of past, present and future mindfully so the "no sense of time" dimension would be contrary which means awareness of the now only or the machine state mind set. In the sense of time dimension one may perceive they are wise because they are aware of the future so they can look ahead and make sure the future is as they want it to be but in reality because their mind is focused on the future what they do in the now is hindered so the future is also hindered because the future is relative to the past and the now. If one is concerned about getting to a party on time, focused on the future, they may overlook the red light that is before them in the now and run the red light and crash and never make it to the party, so to speak. I ran a red light once, so to speak. Planning ahead denotes focusing on the now. If one is not careful or delicate in the now they may not be careful or delicate in the future. The time perception dimension makes one very aware of the past and very aware of the future and thus very blind to the now.

[over the river and through the woods to grandmothers house] is relative to [can't see the forest for the tree's]

[[over the river] = river of Styx = river of anger

[through] = journey

[the woods] = details = parts = Seeing parts is a left brain trait.

[grandmothers house] = safety; security

[can't see] = blind

[forest] = many tree's equal one forest; holistically; everything is one thing a right brain trait.

[the tree's] = parts = details] = To get out of the tree's, the details, one must apply the remedy and then they will cross the river of anger and reach safety, a sound mind, grandmothers house.

When one is born they are conditioned from the forest or holistic perception by the written education into the woods, left brain state so they see parts or details. The devil is the details. Then one applies the remedy and they must cross the river of anger which is a period of "warming up" or becoming accustomed to the normal holistic perception dimension, (You can call it "looking down at the sky" perception dimension if you dislike the word holistic.), and then they are at grandmother's house or safety because one returns to a sound mind again so they are no longer mentally suffering, they escape the place of suffering and place denotes the perception dimension of suffering, having right hemisphere traits veiled, the god image in man, being separated from God. Crossing the river and reaching grandmothers house are rewards for making it out of the woods, the extreme left brain state of mind the education conditions one into.

5/4/2010 5:14:02 AM –

"A good decision is based on knowledge and not on numbers." – Plato

A proper cognitive decision is based on awareness and not money. You would not like Plato. Just about every decision in this narrow is based on money which is numbers. Just about every decision made in this narrow is based on popularity which is numbers. If ten mentally hindered beings make a decision it does not mean it is a proper decision, it only means ten mentally hindered beings see improper decisions as proper decisions.

"It will cost(numbers) too much money(numbers) to educate the children properly so we will educate the children improperly because that is all we can afford(numbers) to do."

"It will cost too much money (numbers) and take too much time (numbers) to educate the children properly so we will educate them swiftly (numbers) and improperly because we can afford (numbers) that education method."

Firstly if one ties money and time to the education of mentally delicate children, one is stupid right off the bat. Stupid people are not allowed to make decisions relative to the delicate minds of children because then the children will become stupid like the said stupid people. The scribes were children with delicate minds that were made stupid by scribes that put money and time (numbers) above the delicate minds of said children and now the children are stupid scribes. If one asks a scribe to make a decision it tends to be a stupid decision because scribes are stupid relative to cognitive ability because of the education and because they never applied the remedy to negate those effects. If you want to live in hell rely on scribes to make decisions. Sense of time is a symptom of a scribe so sense of time is proof of stupidity relative to the scribe's cognitive ability. If you ask a scribe with hindered cognitive ability to make a decision relative to the delicate minds of children they will put money and time (numbers) above the mind of that child and you will end up with a stupid scribe child that senses time. That is what the world is full of now, scribe children that sense time. Scribe children that sense time are making decisions for the young children and in turn are making more scribe children that sense time. Scribe children that sense time are making more scribe children that sense time so the curse caused by the education technology is perpetual.

"All the gold which is under or upon the earth is not enough to give in exchange for virtue." – Plato

Intelligence is not taught and is not bought.

Virtue: the quality of being morally good or righteous.

Scribes that sense time mentally hinder children with their wisdom education so scribes that sense time are perhaps not morally good.

Righteous: always behaving according to a religious or moral code.

"If you keep writing the battle won't start."

X = "What it comes down to is that modern society discriminates against the right hemisphere." - Roger Sperry (1973) Neurobiologist and Nobel Lauriat

Y = "In humans, the frontal lobe reaches full maturity around only after the 20s, marking the cognitive maturity associated with adulthood" - Giedd, Jay N. (october 1999). "Brain Development during childhood and adolescence: a longitudinal MRI study". Nature neuroscience 2 (10): 861-863.

Z = " If you reflect back upon our own educational training, we have been traditionally taught to master the 3 R's: reading, writing and arithmetic -- the domain and strength of the left brain" - The Pitek Group, LLC. Michael P. Pitek, III

Z + Y proves X.

I was a child and scribes that sense time pushed (Y) on me with no foresight into its potential problems and it made my emotions very strong and I eventually became sad and depressed and I could not think clearly and I decided to kill myself but I accidentally mindfully killed myself and negated the damage the education caused me and now I can think clearly and I am dealing with a vast population of scribes that cannot think clearly although the scribes perceive they can think clearly and that is one indication they cannot think clearly. The scribes perceive even after getting all that left brain favoring education as children they are mentally sound and so they have abnormal cognitive ability. The scribes can no longer make reasonable decisions relative to cause and effect relationships.

You are walking down the road and you see ten large men beating a child with clubs. No one else is around and there is no way you can call for help or assistance. (A) If you attack the large men with clubs to attempt to stop them they will kill you with the clubs. (B) If you run like a scared little dog you will be haunted as a result of your timidity, for the rest of infinity.

Being's that have already mindfully killed their self, applied the remedy, tend to pick (A) and beings that have not mindfully killed their self tend to pick (B) and that determination is relative to cognitive ability, foresight and ego. Beings that have mindfully killed their self know and understand what "rest of infinity" means. Beings that have not mindfully killed their self can say "rest of infinity" but do not understand what "rest of infinity" means.

This is how the large men with clubs beat the children to death [reading, writing and arithmetic -- the domain and strength of the left brain]. Because scribes that sense time are timid they will attempt to deny that, perhaps.

Why are scribes stupid? Because they got this [reading, writing and arithmetic -- the domain and strength of the left brain] and did not apply the remedy so they are mentally hindered.

Why does that make them stupid? Because of this ["In humans, the frontal lobe reaches full maturity around only after the 20s, marking the cognitive maturity associated with adulthood"]

Simply put the education mentally hinders the being and until they apply the remedy they are mentally hindered.

Oh author of infinitely poorly disguised thick pamphlet diaries please explain in detail why that makes the stupid scribes stupid scribes.

Grasshopper, the education aborts or stops the child's cognitive development and thus destroys the child mentally and thus destroys the child until the child applies the remedy.

Oh author that shows very little grammatical competence how do we stop the large men that beat the children with the clubs?

One must first stop being one of the large men that beats the children with the clubs.

Oh great author of all authors that have few grammatical skills how do I stop being one of the large men that beat the children with clubs?

One must kill their self mindfully.

Oh great author I am afraid to mindfully kill myself.

Then one must kill their fear so they can kill their self mindfully or one must kill their self mindfully to kill ones fear or timidity.

Oh great author I am not strong enough to do that.

Then one must become submissive so they will not mind the shadow of death.

Oh great author what if I cannot accomplish this mindfully killing myself?

Then one will continue to beat children with clubs.

5/4/2010 10:08:41 AM –

"A good decision is based on knowledge and not on numbers." – Plato

Numerology: the study of the occult use and supposed power of numbers. Numerology is the act of making decisions based on numbers.

A "religious" group may say "All we need is X amount of dollars to continue our ministry", that is numerology. It is making it appear as if when the numbers are "right" then the result will be valid. A disease research group may say "If we can raise 12 million dollars we can cure this disease." So curing the disease is relative to numbers and not knowledge. A government might say "We will raise your taxes 2% and then everything will be fine." A government might say "If we had 50 billion dollars we can solve this economic crisis." This is all numerology and seldom is the end result achieved but often the numbers are achieved. A government might say: " We need more money for the schools to educate the children properly." The problem with that comment is the scribes that sense time do not know what educate means and do not know what properly means but they have the number aspect right. "If the numbers are right everything else will be right." and that is what numerology is. The scribes that sense time have not produced one single human being in five thousand years using their "wisdom" education that is anything but a scribe that senses time unless that being applied the remedy and negates the mental damage the scribe's education caused. That is an absolute. Only after I mindfully killed myself did I achieve consciousness or mental clarity so everything the scribes that sense time pushed on me was in turn negated. When you base your decisions on numbers you no longer are basing your decisions on awareness. Awareness is relative to intuition.

Knowledge: general awareness or possession of information, facts, ideas, truths, or principles.

Number: a figure, symbol, or word used in calculating quantities of individual things.

Numerology is basing decisions on symbols instead of basing decisions on awareness.

Awareness is relative to perception not numbers. In the concept "might makes right", "might" is relative to numbers not perception and thus not awareness and thus not understandings. The scribes that senses time becomes stupid scribes by learning this: [reading, writing and arithmetic] have their right brain intuition, creativity, random access processing, paradox, ambiguity, and complexity veiled or hindered so all they have left to make decisions on are numbers, a left brain aspect, so the scribes that sense time are perhaps nothing but numerologists or sorcerers. Go ask any scribe that senses time, and in this narrow there are many, about anything and eventually numbers will come up. "We don't have enough money to do that." "It will cost lots of money to do that.", "If I had money I could make a difference." The scribes that sense time are sorcerers or cultists. The scribes that sense time cannot do anything unless the numbers are right. A scribe that senses time will go to a job interview and if the numbers are not right they will say "They did not pay me enough so the numbers were not right." The scribes that sense time determine value by numbers and that is numerology. "How many years of education did you get because that will determine the amount (number) in wages (numbers) we will pay you." It is all based on numbers. Determinations based on numbers is numerology. "Your IQ is not high enough", based on numbers."How many children do you have?", based on numbers. "Let's get a census calculation." , based on numbers. Democracy itself is based on numbers and therefore it is not based on understandings or wisdom. You ask ten scribes that sense time to vote on something and you will always get "ten scribes that vote on something" results. Budgets are based on numbers so budgets are not based on understandings or awareness but simply numerology. A number will never protect you or keep you safe but awareness and cognitive ability will. If all one is doing is making determinations based on numbers one is a numerologist. That is not good or bad it just is. A scribe that senses time does not want to face the fact they are nothing but a sorcerer and a numerologist and thus an occult practitioner because then that means they are not wise. "Let's check the numbers." That is what a numerologist does. It has nothing to do with wisdom or awareness it is just a premise that numbers are of greater value than awareness or wisdom. A scribe that senses time will say "Yes but we needed numbers to get to the moon.' But that scribe that senses time does not realize the only reason they want to go to the moon is to make money (numbers) by exploiting any resources (numbers) they may find there. Resources appear as numbers to scribes that sense time. In infinity there are only two numbers, zero and infinity so any number that is not infinity is zero. The devil is in the details and the details are all the numbers in between zero and infinity. Zero is "no beginning" and infinity is "no end." A scribe that senses time cannot function without numbers because numbers are their God. The scribes that sense time have a four headed ram god. They may not know it is a four headed ram god because they are scribes that sense time. I beat four headed ram gods to death with my words accidentally. I am not better than scribes that sense time I am simply completely opposite of the scribes that sense time. I do not mentally destroy innocent children starting at the age of six and the scribes love to mentally destroy innocent children starting at the age of six and they force me to support their actions using their fear tactics because they know not what they do. I do not mentally rape children and the scribes that sense time love to mentally rape children and they like to keep track using numbers of how many they mentally rape and when the numbers are not right they find ways to mentally rape the innocent children more efficiently. Efficiency is relative to numbers. I am mindful of other beings that have partially mindfully killed their self and they become scared little dogs when they see how many scribes that sense time there are. The stock market is based on nothing but numbers. Some scribes that sense time invest in the stock market when the numbers are good and thus they are just numerologists. Scribes that sense time have trouble letting go of things because everything they do is based on numbers. If the numbers are not right a scribe that senses time will give up.

Peace: a calm and quiet state, free from disturbances or noise.

Peace is a symptom one's mind no longer works. Peace is a symptom one got mentally raped into hell at the hands of the scribes that sense time. Peace is a symptom ones god is a four headed ram god and I beat four headed ram gods to death with my words, accidentally.

War: a serious struggle, argument, or conflict between people.

Serious: very great, bad, dangerous, harmful, or difficult to handle.

You are a container in a serious struggle that is dangerous and difficult to handle so you need your mind at full power and the only way you can get your mind back at this stage is to mindfully kill yourself because the scribes that sense time mentally raped you into hell with their "brand" of education. There are no morals when innocent children are being mentally hindered into hell by scribes that sense time so get that into your pinprick mind. There are no rules when innocent children are being mentally raped into hell by scribes that sense time. You are in the war, it is just a matter of what side you want to be on. There is not going to be an encore so do not save anything for the encore.

[Jonah 4:4 Then said the LORD, Doest thou well to be angry?]

[Then said the LORD] = Out of sequence. A signpost of authenticity. Should be [Then the Lord said] so the being that wrote this texts was dyslexic meaning they have the right brain random access aspect in their conscious state of mind and so they appeared dyslexic not on the level of letters but on the level of words relative to sentence structure.

24

5/4/2010 2:59:06 PM –

[Genesis 2:17 But of the tree of the knowledge of good and evil, thou shalt not eat of it: for in the day that thou eatest thereof thou shalt surely die.]

A = [the tree of the knowledge] = [reading, writing and arithmetic]

B = [thou shalt surely die(mindfully and on a species level).]

Fact: You got (A).

Fact: Now you have to (B).

It is important to discuss how you are going to mindfully kill yourself because that is paramount to everything relative to the universe. Breathing is not more important than you mindfully dying. You are either going to mindfully die or you are going to suffer and I am pleased if you wish to suffer. After I convince you to mindfully kill yourself your eyes are going to be opened and the very first thing you are going to understand is you are alive. The next thing you are going to understand is that modern society mentally raped you into hell and you are a rape victim. The next thing you are going to understand is modern society mentally rapes everyone into hell as children with their "wisdom" education and you are simply a rape victim that is aware they got raped, and many are not aware of that. So my purpose is to convince you to mindfully kill yourself because you are mindfully dead and the only way a dead person can come back to life is to kill their self mindfully and although the language is flawed and you perhaps cannot grasp that concept, it is truth.

Necromancer: the practice of attempting to communicate with the spirits of the dead.

One might suggest you are quite difficult to communicate with. You hold onto death because you think it is life. My purpose is to convince you that you are dead. You do not want me to convince you that you are mindfully dead but what you want does not matter because you are pleased with your mindful death you perceive is mindful life. You can look at it from a psychological point of view, a neurological point of view or a spiritual point of view but when it comes down it you are going to mindfully kill yourself. In necromancy often things go wrong and often times the dead become more dead in the process and not only am I willing to live with that reality I am indifferent to it. I do not fear the dead and you are dead. The good news is once I convince you to mindfully kill yourself you will become a necromancer and the bad news is you will never be as poor at necromancy as me. Necromancy is not very popular in the pit of dead so many hide their profession. I don't hide my profession because quite frankly the dead are plenty stupid to begin with, that's why they are dead.

This is what mindfully hindered you or mindfully killed you:

A = [the tree of the knowledge] = [reading, writing and arithmetic]

And this is what will bring you back to life.

B = [thou shalt surely die.]

It is a little late for you to be worrying about why someone would mindfully kill you. You don't want to believe this mindfully killed you:

A = [the tree of the knowledge] = [reading, writing and arithmetic]

You will want to suspend what you call "your intelligence" for a moment because if you were not dead I would not be attempting to raise you from the dead. It is impossible to raise something that is alive back to life so you cannot be alive and that means you are dead. I don't have to disguise my agenda because you are dead. You don't want me to raise you from the dead but that is all I do. I raise the dead because I have nothing else to do that challenges me. I don't care if I don't raise anyone from the dead it is still a challenge and it's give me my daily bread, something to ponder. Some might say raising the dead is impossible but that is all I do. I would rather not raise the dead but the dead keep making more dead. I raise the dead and I don't care what their name is. It is not polite to take money from dead people so you can keep your money. I have nothing else to do but raise the dead and that is payment enough. You cannot raise a necromancer from the dead but you are free to try. Now that we understand each other I am going to go about my business.

5/4/2010 4:36:31 PM –

An insignificant failure is an impressive adversary. You will never get lost once you understand all roads are roads. As your friends increase your opinions decrease. Decision's made based on awareness is wisdom; decisions made based on numbers is numerology.

Meditating in a hurricane requires discipline; meditating in your home requires snack chips.

If you think about a battery in a tape recorder, when the battery gets low the tape won't play or the tape will play slow so the music sounds distorted. The battery still has a charge but you know the batteries are dead when the music will no longer play. So your mind is that dead battery. Your mind still has a charge but it won't play so your mental clarity is distorted until you get recharged.

This drained all the life from your mind. [the tree of the knowledge] = [reading, writing and arithmetic]. The only way you will recharge the battery is if you understand your battery is dead and my name is "convince you that you are dead." I am not a timid necromancer and that means I do not give half charges I only give full charges. If you want a half charge you can go find a timid necromancer and get your half charge and you can be their little slave dog for the rest of infinity. My name is not half charge and that means I cut out 100% of the dead right off the bat. Simply put I don't have to raise you from the dead so I do it for folly and since I do it for folly I go all the way. I am not concerned who you think you are, who your friends think you are or who society thinks you are. If you sense time you are nothing but a dead battery to me. I don't do lukewarm I only have one setting, infinite hot. The only prayer you are going to be saying from here on out is this one:

[Jonah 4:3 Therefore now, O LORD, take, I beseech thee, my life from me; for it is better for me to die than to live.]

28

You are this: [Psalms 31:12 I am forgotten as a dead man out of mind: I am like a broken vessel.]

Although you are a broken vessel because of this: [the tree of the knowledge] = [reading, writing and arithmetic]; I am a potter. I am an unorthodox potter.

Unorthodox: failing to follow conventional or traditional beliefs or practices.

You may think life is pleasing and life is fun and life is joyous but that is only because your eyes have been sown shut. Do you think Jonah was kidding when he prayed this prayer?

[Jonah 4:3 Therefore now, O LORD, take, I beseech thee, my life from me; for it is better for me to die than to live.]

Jonah was asking God to kill him and not because he had done anything wrong it was because he had done something right. Jonah saw very clearly what was happening in this narrow and he said "Kill me please."

Beseech: to ask earnestly or beg somebody to do something.

Jonah was begging for death yet it was because he had done something proper or right. You may pray for wisdom but that is only because you are blind and you may pray for sight but that is only because you are a fool. If you were intelligent you would pray for death. Jonah was intelligent and he begged for death. Jonah could see very clearly where he was at. When you are begging God to kill you with all of your might you know where you are at. When you are begging God to kill you with all of your might you know your eyes are open. My purpose is to make sure your eyes are opened. My purpose is to make Jonah 4:3 your mantra for the rest of infinity.

Mantra: an expression or idea that is repeated, often without thinking about it, and closely associated with something.

Now there are some that will show you a little light but I am going to burn your eyes right out of their sockets. The first thing you are going to think is: "I should have never invaded that beings private diaries". The second thing you are going to think is "Why are my eyes burned out of their sockets?" And the third thing you are going to think is Jonah 4:3. The problem is our species has killed itself with this: [reading, writing and arithmetic]. As a collective relative to a species we are dead. I don't see any hope at all. If you wish to go read Winnie the Pooh now I welcome you to it. You don't understand what I am saying but this being understands what I am saying :

[reading, writing and arithmetic] = [S. B. (20) committed suicide by gunshot - Jan 03, 2010]

That is the fruit of the tree of knowledge. The tree reaps what it sow's. One might suggest it spreads its seed awful thick in this narrow.

5/5/2010 8:48:38 AM – [Psalms 88:5 Free among the dead, like the slain that lie in the grave, whom thou rememberest no more: and they are cut off from thy hand.]

[Free among the dead] = Free are the ones that restore their mind after they eat off the tree of knowledge

30

using the remedy and they return to being free spirits. The dead are the ones that eat off the tree of knowledge and do not apply the remedy to restore their mind, the ones that sense time, the scribes.

[like the slain that lie in the grave] This is referring to the "dead" and then it says: [they are cut off from thy hand]. Thy hand is the right hemisphere and this turns those aspects off: [the tree of the knowledge] = [reading, writing and arithmetic]. The scribes are not slightly insane, in fact their cognitive ability has been totally aborted by the education and they are really beyond the insane. They are so insane they cannot even tell they are insane at all. The fact the scribes have medicine to attempt to remedy this education induced insanity is proof of the insanity. The reason dead is used so often in the ancient texts is to explain the scribes because the insanity is not curable for the vast majority.

[they are cut off from thy hand.] For the vast majority of human beings that got all that left brain favoring education long before their delicate mind was even developed they are cut off.

[Genesis 3:14   And the LORD God said unto the serpent, Because thou hast done this, thou art cursed above all cattle, and above every beast of the field; upon thy belly shalt thou go, and dust shalt thou eat all the days of thy life:]

[Because thou hast done this(got the education technology), thou art cursed above all cattle(have right brain traits veiled),... all the days of thy life(it is very hard to apply the remedy relative to a timid scribe):]

The scribes are mentally killing innocent children and are not even aware of it and doing it far beyond the numbers of any war and far beyond the numbers that one can even perhaps understand. Not one hundred million but billions upon billions. The scribes do this [cut off from thy hand.] to billions of people because the scribes are this [they are cut off from thy hand.] The scribes are cut off from the hand of god, right hemisphere, the god image in man, because they ate off the tree of knowledge and didn't apply the remedy, keep the covenant, so there is nothing they can do but destroy and kill everything in their path and that is all they do and what adds insult to injury is they do not even believe they do that and they are not even aware they do that and so it gives one the impression they are possessed by some sort of sinister aspect far beyond mans ability to even grasp. I wonder why your cult leader has not told you that by now. I wonder why your cult leader would keep that information from you if they were aware of it. You hold onto your desire to believe the "supernatural is coming to save me" aspect because you do not want to go down the road called "you got mentally hindered into hell as a child". You do not want to go down that road and I do not blame you. I am not writing these volumes because the scribes got mentally hindered as children, I am writing these volumes because the scribes are mentally hindering children. The scribes are cutting the innocent little ones off from the hand with the tree of knowledge and that is not tolerated. In the Sistine chapel there is the hand of god, right hemisphere and the scribes are the ones reaching for the hand of god yet you cannot reach it because they are cut off from the hand of god, right hemisphere.

Tolerated: to be willing to allow something to happen or exist.

I am not willing.

X = [reading, writing and arithmetic].

Y = remedy to X

Z = population of species that does not get X

A = population of species that does get X

B = population of species that does get X and also applies the remedy

C = extinction

D = species population

E = offspring

X + D = A

(Z < A) + (B < A) = C

X + D = C

If you take any species and cut the right hemisphere out of their brain they are factually going to go extinct. It is logical they perhaps will either kill off their environment or kill their self off by killing off their environment. I do not detect ghosts or lizard men are coming to save us.

A is the majority and B is the minority. A is making the decisions and so the offspring are going to be converted to A.

(A) is insane so it is logical they would take(E)the offspring and make them insane also using (X)and not even be aware of it at all and that is why they are insane from (X). Eventually as a species, if (X) is not identified as a potential serious mental health problem we are going to see a window and jump out thinking we can fly. For example we are concerned about the economy and going to mars and finding more oil and at the exact same time we are mentally hindering all the offspring and we do not even think that is what we are doing at all. As a species we are concerned about things that are totally irrelevant considering the fact as a species we are destroying all the offspring mentally. It has never been about anything but one simple reality. This [X =   [reading, writing and arithmetic]] kills human beings mentally and because the remedy is quite difficult to apply relative to a timid being the damage is permanent.

I am not really use to infinity yet and at the same time it seems like I have been here for infinity.

5/6/2010 8:04:43 AM -

X = [reading, writing and arithmetic].

Y = remedy to Z

Z = schizophrenic caused by learning X

D = cured of schizophrenia caused by X

C = child

X + C = Z

Z + Y = D

The nature of the education induced schizophrenia is fear and timidity so the remedy is to condition the being out of the fear and timidity to an absolute

34

degree but because the being is fearful and timid they will resist that and assume it is wise to resist and therefore the being may never be cured. The cure is not to overcome some fears, the cure is to overcome the greatest fear and that is fear of perceived death. In a situation where a being in the schizophrenia is given a choice to run and save their self when their mind says "Death is certain if you do not run or take action" the being tends to run or take action. So the timidity caused by the schizophrenia nearly ensures the being will never be cured of the schizophrenia. The fear and timidity is what is affecting the beings cognitive ability and that hindered cognitive ability is keeping the being from being able to apply the remedy or cure the schizophrenia. The schizophrenic must rely on their own decisions to apply the remedy and their decisions are not sound or reliable. The schizophrenic must rely on their own instinct to apply the cure yet they cannot rely on their own instinct and thus they may not apply the cure.

G = society

E = [reading, writing and arithmetic].

F = free will

H = remedy

J = schizophrenia

G + E = J

J + E = G

J + F > H

It is probable a schizophrenic given free will may choose schizophrenia over sanity. Society is schizophrenic and so given free will it is probable they will choose to make their own offspring schizophrenic. A being out of touch with reality, and in this case in a timid and fearful perception reality, must not associate, while considering applying the remedy, with beings that are timid and fearful because if they are in contact with beings that are timid or fearful it is probable that will cause them to become more timid and fearful. Relative to the perception of a timid and fearful being, a fearless being appears dangerous. A timid and fearful being will surrender many things such as rights and freedom just to achieve a perceived state of safety and this is because they tend to make their decisions based on fear and timidity. This means it is probable the schizophrenic will live out their life making decisions not based on logic or sound reasoning but based on perceived safety. It is not logical to give a child years of left brain favoring education starting when the child is six considering their mind is very delicate at that age but it is safe relative to the schizophrenics perception. Another way to look at it is making sure the children get that left brain favoring education is a safe bet but not a logical or reasonable bet. There was a President that said something along the lines of "If you want to be safe just go to prison." So you were a child and your parents wanted to be safe and so they gave you the education with no foresight to its possible mental implications because all their friends were giving the education to their children and if your parents did not follow suit they would be "outcasts in the herd" and that is a fearful place to be relative to a timid being, and now you are in prison and I am the prison warden. There are beings alive now and beings in the ancient

36

texts who are convinced after eating off that tree of knowledge the scribes are the devil. The devil cannot reason and scribes cannot reason. Some suggest never reason with a demon because a demon cannot reason. I give everyone the benefit of the doubt meaning I at least explain the remedy to everyone. Maybe you are going to look at yourself and adjust the errors of your ways and attempt to question written education and math relative to their effects on the mind of young children, or maybe you are going to spit at me and opt for the red sea route. There is a problem with these words I arrange that you should be aware of. I am explaining things to the species that only beings with slight emotional capacity should hear. That means it is probable if certain beings that sense time read these texts they may not be able to emotionally handle what is suggested and they may go as you put it "ballistic". That is not my problem that is the scribes problem because I don't fear death. I factually do not care one way or another. I have no guilt. I have no shame. I have no pride. I have no ego. The scribes will attempt to make it look like I am in the wrong or I am doing the improper thing by suggesting the remedy to the tree of knowledge. I sit in my isolation chamber taunting a rabid animal. Early after the accident I was positive and hopeful because I was not aware of the rabid animal. The sinister has some very noteworthy aspects and one of them is it cannot reason.

"A good decision is based on knowledge and not on numbers." – Plato

The sinister will create a list of the children that do the best at the education technology and number them in order of importance. The sinister will call the list the honor roll. The children that do the best at the, god image in man veiling tool you know as education will be high on the list, the honor roll list.

Honor: great respect and admiration.

So the children that veil the god image in man, right hemisphere, the best by doing the best at the left brain favoring education are respected and admired the most by the cult of the four headed ram god you call modern society. So the little children that hate the god image in man the most, are rewarded by being on top of the list called the honor roll. The children that demonstrate willingness to discriminate the god image in man the most are respected and admired by the scribe rulers. The little children that hate the god image in man the most (good grades) are respected the most and the little children that resist hating the god image in man(bad grades) may not even make the honor roll list at all and in turn they are discriminated against by the ruler scribes and society itself. The ruler scribes put "in God we trust" on their money and then they reward the little children that show willingness to hate God the most with a high ranking on their honor roll list. The little children that make that list have a mark of honor, they are honored for hating God in this narrow. I do not expect a scribe to understand that because they not only hate God, they hate an entire hemisphere of their mind and in turn hate their self and most importantly they hate the very little ones that still have that hemisphere working. The darkness will understand it is darkness in the presence of light and that is evident in what the scribes do to the little ones. The scribes are great in number but that does not mean their intelligence or wisdom is great in number. The scribes are timid and afraid and that is how one defeats them, with fear. That is a risky business because the scribes come to conclusions based on fear. A parent scribe will fear for that child if that child does not make it on that honor roll list and a scribe parent will feel safe if their child does make it on that honor roll list. A scribe parent will put a sticker on their car that says "My child made the honor list" and in turn tell the universe that their child hates God and the god image in man more than anyone's child does. That parent scribe using that sticker is telling the universe "I am a proud parent of a God hating child and I am dam proud of it." That scribe parent is saying " You wish your child hated the god image in man, right hemisphere, as much as I have taught my own child to hate the god image in man and thus God." Since my purpose is to beat the hell out of bullies with my words accidentally I am pleased with that prospect. I am pleased there are so many bumper stickers in this infinity that say "My child is an honor roll student." Perhaps I am truly blessed perhaps. Happiness is relative to awareness as grief is relative to comprehension.

5/6/2010 4:24:06 PM – Drips - http://www.youtube.com/watch?v=fOWYLDu77Z4

Drip by drip the container fills.
Drop by drop the contents swell.
Containment dome you have to leave home.
The risks are underestimated
I'm lucky to be alive
I'm lucky to attack the hive.
You'll get the latest updates, prorates, obey announcements.
You'll get the boozy gaga, choosey ha ha, the concerted la la.

You'll get released from the hospital because your
cancer is hospitable
But don't come near me because I already ate
Refuse to be tamed, deny your fame
Stop listening to me
You have your own rotten tree
Ten lessons your should learn
Privacy flaw is the burn
New dating site
Last season's light
You'll get the latest updates, prorates, obey
announcements.
You'll get the boozy gaga, choosey ah ha, the
concerted la la.
You'll get the latest updates, prorates, obey
announcements.
You'll get the boozy gaga, choosey ha ha, the
concerted la la.
You'll get the
You'll get the drips.
*

Depression is achieved when a being is aware something
is wrong but cannot fully comprehend what. Faith is
intuition with purpose. Wisdom is just past the end of
the rope. The harshest absolute is absolute probability.

*

In zero land the wind will guide
To drift and then pulled to the side
The breeze would not lift the shroud
Though commanded not allowed
Outside the crowd resisted still

Consider growth, ignore the will
Empty from the strangled vine
All is shown once on the line
Ones could stretch unbroken thread
Define the limits of those not fed.
The number would not show them much
The judgments caused by factors such
The ocean could not pay that debt
Although I would not place a bet
Write a letter to no one.
Let it float into the sun
Hide away from walls built up
What wealth would come from empty cup?
They would not say why they resist
The vacant lot or broken list
Pretend they would to see unknown
The breeze would not lift the shroud
The rose of bliss withered now
Consumed beneath by dirty plough.
*

Some music would not sound the same
Inclined to hear what should not find
In the thoughts of willing night
Certain notes bring certain fright
Nature does not sell its soul
Although the others would not show
Wisdom does not care for much
Only grit from misplaced steps
*

5/7/2010 7:45:26 AM – Watching a documentary about quantum mechanics they were talking about the fact two scientists who won Nobel prizes for discovering contrary aspect's. One being proved that an electron is a wave and one being proved an electron is a particle and they both won Nobel prizes for each discovery.

Wave: an oscillation that travels through a medium by transferring energy from one particle or point to another without causing any permanent displacement of the medium.

Particle: a unit of matter smaller than the atom or its main components.

One being in the documentary said "If we sat down and thought about what the implications of these discoveries really meant we may not get anything done." Another way to look at it is, if you think you are doing something you must be doing something although you perhaps are not doing anything. I do not register mentally I am writing books because I am awake and am fully aware I am not doing anything at all and you may read these books and perceive I am doing something and you are right also. So I am writing these books and not writing these books at the exact same time. It is complex because it indicates as a species we have been mentally hindered so we are trying very hard to do something when we perhaps cannot do anything. Modern society is going through very many steps to get back to where the tribes that live in nature are right now. Another way to look at it is, the tribes that live in nature and do not have written language and math is where modern society is headed towards but may become extinct first, so modern society is not doing anything but attempting in a very prolonged way to get back to where they were five thousand years ago mindfully. Another way to look at it is modern society is attempting to become sound minded human beings again and it is taking them five thousand years to do that but it is probable they are going to wipe everyone out in the process and never achieve that. The scribes want there to be purpose so they look at all of these details they are great at seeing and say "Certainly there is purpose because all of these details prove it." but once they apply the remedy and restore their mind they will no longer see the details and thus they will no longer detect purpose. Quantum mechanics is in fact attempts by human beings that have been conditioned into an alternate level of consciousness, a dimension, by the tree of knowledge trying to get out of that alternate dimension. The proof is, they are starting to discover paradox.

An electron is a particle and an electron is a wave is a paradox and suggests there are perhaps no absolutes and that means whatever you think is happening is probably and probably not happening at the exact same time. That appears to be crazy but it is a symptom of what happens in a true vacuum or a void. We eat food and we keep breathing and we keep breathing and we eat food but that is not an absolute it is simply a probability which means it is possible it is not happening. Einstein was very big on time which means he was aware time is relative and perhaps the only way a person could understand time was relative or time varies depending on location or depending on the observer would be if a person had no sense of time. When a person has a strong sense of time , time is very real and when a person has no sense of time, time is vague. This perception is like a mirror. You are looking into a mirror and you sense time and the image in the mirror has no sense of time and your goal is to convince that image that there is time but when you say "There is time" to that image the image responds with the exact opposite comment "There is no time."

So this mirror image is attempting to convince you there is no time and you are attempting to convince the image there is time and both observations are correct at the exact same time. You are saying "There is purpose and I have purpose" and the mirror image is saying "There is no purpose and I have no purpose" and both observations are right at the exact same time. This probability aspect suggests there is a universe and that only means it is possible there isn't and that is what quantum mechanics is a science of, probability. It is probable you are alive which means it is possible you are nothing but a thought making observations. Is a thought a wave or a particle? It is probable a thought is a wave and a particle which means it is possible it is neither. The tree of knowledge has altered our minds into an alternate perception dimension and so we are in fact out of touch with reality and we exhibit traits of being out of touch with reality but at the same time science in its quests to "progress" is in fact just moving closer to where we were at before science was even invented. A person is born and if that person sat in one spot their entire life and did nothing at all except ate food and water to stay alive they would accomplish exactly what a person that runs around attempting to do things accomplishes.

X = circle

Y = square

Z = observation

A = reality

B = being that senses time

C = being with no sense of time

B + Z = X

C + Z = Y

A = XY or A = YX

So this shows a circle is not a circle and a square is not a square in reality but a circle is a circle and a square is a square when they are observed and this is what probability is and that is what quantum mechanics is, probably. Human beings decided using thoughts(decisions) to make an atom bomb and they did but was it because they harnessed the power of the atom or was it because they thought they could? It is probable an atom has lots of energy that can be released under certain circumstances which means it is possible it does not. It is probable you are reading this sentence which means it is possible you are not. A being finishes their work or a job and they think "I am tired because I finished that job.", but they only perceive they finished that job and so they perceive they are tired. If a person wakes up from sleeping and lay's in bed all day and does nothing they will perceive they accomplished nothing that day. If the person that laid in bed all day had the thoughts from the person that finished that job placed in their mind that person although they still laid in bed all day would still feel tired because they perceive they just finished a job. We are exactly what we want to be. As a species we can say "We do not want to mentally hinder children by pushing years of left brain favoring education on their delicate minds." But that is what we are doing so that is what we want to do. We want to hurt ourselves because the education has made us out of touch with reality or altered our perceptions and so we perceive education is helping children on an absolute scale but it is really harming children on an absolute scale because our minds signals are crossed from the education. We know not what we do. Another way to look at it is we are doing exactly what we want to do but we are out of touch with reality so what we want to do is the reverse of what we are doing. I saw a commercial and a woman said "Since our children are the future we owe it to them to give them the best education possible." What that woman was really saying is "Since our children are the future we owe it to them to harm them as much as possible mentally so we will not have a future using the flawed education technology." That women may say "That is not what I said" and that proves he is out of touch with reality and that is what schizophrenia is. The education technology factually hinders the delicate mind of a child and if all of society says it does not it proves all of society is out of touch with reality and thus schizophrenic because they got the education technology. The scribes fruits and deeds reveal their nature. Modern society factually discriminates against right hemisphere on a horrendous scale and factually does not think they do so they are factually out of touch with reality and thus factually schizophrenic.

"Since our children are the future we owe it to them to give them the best education possible." This comment is suicide. It is saying if we kill the future we will not have a future and that is what a suicidal person is mindful of, making sure there is no future.

X = alternate perception dimension

Y = normal perception dimension

Everything X says is the reverse of what they mean. Everything Y says is the reverse of what X understands

46

to be true. I am suggesting it is probable there are some problems pushing that left brain favoring education on the minds of young children and you are perhaps thinking it is absolutely impossible that could be true. You think it is perhaps absolutely impossible because if it is even probable then you got mentally harmed and it is not probable you are capable of eating such a large plate of crow in your alternate perception dimension state of mind. As a species we are getting what we ask for except what we ask for is the reverse of what we are getting because as a species we keep conditioning each other into an alternate perception dimension so we perceive the reverse. Simply put as a species our wires are crossed. We ask for cold water and get hot water but drink it and perceive it is cold water.

You say " I want to give my child a better education than I got." And you mean "I want to harm my child more than I got harmed." But you do not believe that because your wires are crossed because your parents said "I want my child to get a better education than I got." which means they harmed you also because their wires were crossed by the education technology You want to harm children because you were harmed as a child and it is as simple as that. Yes it is unfortunate you were mentally hindered and thus abused as a child by the education at the request of the adult scribes but that is no excuse to harm children as you were harmed. You want peace which means you want war. You want to live which means you want to die. You want to get along which means you want to fight. You want to be left alone which means you want to control. You want freedom which means you want tyranny. You don't want a blood bath which means you love blood baths. If you love death it means you love life and the suicidal scribes love death and they are the only ones of value in my infinity.

[Luke 17:33 ..; and whosoever shall lose his life (mindfully) shall preserve it.]

After all that education if you are not suicidal you are not a probabale canidate for the remedy. You want to cure the suicidal which means you do not want them to return to mental life. You say you understand which proves you do not understand. You say you are religious which proves you are not religious. You say you love peace which proves you love war. You say you do not harm children which proves you love to harm children. What do you think the common people are going to do to a being that loves to harm children knowingly or unknowingly to the degree it is second nature for them to harm children?

I am explaining to common people on a world wide scale this:

X = "What it comes down to is that modern society discriminates against the right hemisphere." - Roger Sperry (1973) Neurobiologist and Nobel Lauriat

Y = "In humans, the frontal lobe reaches full maturity around only after the 20s, marking the cognitive maturity associated with adulthood" - Giedd, Jay N. (october 1999). "Brain Development during childhood and adolescence: a longitudinal MRI study". Nature neuroscience 2 (10): 861-863.

Z = " If you reflect back upon our own educational training, we have been traditionally taught to master the 3 R's: reading, writing and arithmetic -- the domain

and strength of the left brain" -The Pitek Group, LLC.
Michael P. Pitek, III

You love to give the children (Z) and because of (Y)
you love to mentally harm children and thus physically
harm children and you love to do it and you love it
so much it has become second nature for you to harm
children.

You are modern society and you mentally harm children
and I was one of them and I escaped your abuse and now
the abused has become the abuser and you have a tattoo
on your forehead that says "Please abuse me first." Do
you not see that tattoo because I see it clearly and I am
pleased with that prospect. I am blessed because all I
see are beings with tattoo's on their forehead that say
"Please author with no grammatical skills abuse me
first." If you think it is probable (X) and (Y) are probable
then it is probable your longevity is not probable.
Pleased to meet you. Hope you guess my name.

X = "What it comes down to is that modern society
discriminates against the right hemisphere." - Roger
Sperry (1973) Neurobiologist and Nobel Lauriat

Y = "In humans, the frontal lobe reaches full maturity
around only after the 20s, marking the cognitive
maturity associated with adulthood" - Giedd, Jay N.
(october 1999). "Brain Development during childhood
and adolescence: a longitudinal MRI study". Nature
neuroscience 2 (10): 861-863.

Z = " If you reflect back upon our own educational training, we have been traditionally taught to master the 3 R's: reading, writing and arithmetic -- the domain and strength of the left brain" -
The Pitek Group, LLC.
Michael P. Pitek, III

Z + Y = X

When a little child has all of this [reading, writing and arithmetic] pushed on them starting at the age of six and considering their cognitive ability does not mature until they are in their 20's = [the frontal lobe reaches full maturity around only after the 20s] It means traditional education mentally aborts children and so in the ancient texts this [reading, writing and arithmetic] was called the tree of knowledge.

The tree of knowledge was thought to make one wise. [Genesis 3:6   and a tree to be desired to make one wise]

Traditional education, [reading, writing and arithmetic], is thought to make one wise.

So it is a well disguised Trojan horse. The truth is, because traditional education favors left hemisphere so much it in turn veils right hemisphere traits like creativity, complexity, intuition and random access processing it in fact mentally hinders a person or makes them stupid. If one woke up tomorrow in a world of six billion beings on PCP and one saw them doing many

"PCP' like deeds one would be very timid unless one had no timidity. That concept perhaps demonstrates the wise beings in the ancient texts had no timidity because we have the ancient texts. This suggests some beings that apply this remedy fully may keep their mouth shut because they may perceive it is not exactly wise to excite a great number of chaff by insulting their education technology.

And thus the comment:
[Jeremiah 8:8 How do ye say, We are wise, and the law of the LORD is with us? Lo, certainly in vain made he it; the pen of the scribes is in vain.]

How do ye say, We are wise, and the law of the LORD is with us? How can a person say the Lord is with them when the God image in man is the right hemisphere and the tree of knowledge veils that aspect unless they apply the remedy?

Imhotep is the patron saint of scribes. He was an Egyptian commoner, not a Pharaoh, that became very popular because of his ability to create charms, which is what you would know as wise proverbs. So Imhotep who lived about 4500 years ago made these wise sayings and plastered them all over and slowly people starting reading them or wanting to read them and so people started conditioning their self into the "extreme left brain state".

According to myth, Imhotep's mother was a mortal named *Kheredu-ankh*, elevated later to semi-divine status by claims that she was the daughter of Banebdedet, a four headed ram god. So the scribes god is a four headed ram god and a scribe that applies the remedy leaves that cult and returns to the "ONE" god relative to holistic perception.

So this comment:

X = "What it comes down to is that modern society discriminates against the right hemisphere." - Roger Sperry (1973) Neurobiologist and Nobel Lauriat

Is saying in spirit: Modern society, the cult of the four headed ram god, discriminates against the god image in man, right hemisphere.

Of course Sigmund Freud said "Neurosis is the inability to tolerate ambiguity"

Ambiguity is a right brain trait. Jesus had moments of doubt or ambiguity. Thus when he was compared to other people they said this of him.

[Mark 1:22 And they were astonished at his doctrine: for he taught them as one that had authority, and not as the scribes.]

[for he (Jesus) taught them as one that had authority, and not as the scribes(the ones in this cult of the four headed ram god).]

If one combines the two comments, Freud's and Sperry's:

"Neurosis is the inability to tolerate ambiguity": "What it comes down to is that modern society discriminates against the right hemisphere."

What is comes down to is the neurotics, modern society, discriminate or cannot tolerate right hemisphere including traits such as ambiguity.

That is a nice way of saying the darkness see's the light (the children with perfect minds) as darkness and must kill the light(the children's minds) because the light (the children) reveal to the darkness(the scribes) what the darkness is.

So this comment is saying in spirit:
[for he (Jesus) taught them as one that had authority, and not as the scribes(the ones in the cult of the four headed ram god).]

Jesus was the Lord or Master of the house(sound minded) because he applied the remedy and the anti-christ was the scribes because it is saying Jesus was not like the scribes or anti to the ways of the scribes , and that is why John wrote:

[1 John 2:18 Little children, it is the last time: and as ye have heard that antichrist shall come, even now are there many antichrists; whereby we know that it is the last time.]

John was saying in spirit, little children beware of the scribes, they are the antichirst and they are great in number and they are going to push their "tree of knowledge" on you and give you the mark, mark's are what written letters where called in ancient Egypt not letters and that is why this comment was made:

[Luke 20:46 Beware of the scribes, which desire to walk in long robes, and love greetings in the markets, and the highest seats in the synagogues, and the chief rooms at feasts;]

[1 John 2:18 Little children [Beware of the scribes] even now are there many antichrists.]

[Romans 10:9 That if thou shalt confess with thy mouth the Lord Jesus, and shalt believe in thine heart that God hath raised him from the dead, thou shalt be saved.]

This comment is why beings that have not applied the remedy cannot understand the ancient texts because they require complexity to understand. Simple minded left brain linear, "take everything on face value" mental processing is not going to cut it, so to speak.

Lord Jesus is the same thing as Master Jesus relative to Master of the house relative to a being with a sound mind who has applied the remedy and thus understands the remedy and thus can explain the remedy to the tree of knowledge.

[raised him from the dead] This is simply saying, if you believe Jesus applied the remedy and became a Lord then you will at least believe him when he explained the remedy, and the remedy is:

[Luke 17:33 ; and whosoever shall lose his life (mindfully) shall preserve it.]

[Luke 9:23 And he said to them all, If any man will come after me, [let him deny himself], and take up his cross daily, and follow me.]

Don't say you believe in Jesus and you believe he was raised from the dead and then not apply the remedy he suggested because then I have to write in the volumes you are a blind fool that knows not what you say or do. Sayings words means nothing in contrast to applying the remedy, and the remedy means everything in this narrow. If you rely on stupid false teachers you will end up stupid and false. You get to say you believe in Jesus after you apply the remedy he suggested and not a moment before. You say the words but you do not back it up with anything so it is all just hot air.

[Luke 17:33 ; and whosoever shall lose his life (mindfully) shall preserve it.]

Achieving this remedy is your goal in life because you ate off the tree of knowledge and until you apply this remedy you are dead mindfully. You are skipping to the "preserve it" part and you are overlooking the "lose his life mindfully" part. You factually cannot get the preserve it part until you factually lose your life mindfully. It is an "If.. Then" statement.

If [you lose your life (mindfully)] then [you preserve your mental life], which means you restore the god image in man, your right hemisphere after the tree of knowledge veiled it. If anyone in the universe tells you that is not true then you will know they are a false. Now you can go anywhere in the universe and say "Those that lose their life mindfully preserve it" and if anyone says "That is not truth" you will know they are anti-truth. It is quite simple, a being that has applied the remedy cannot say the remedy is not true and a being that has not applied the remedy cannot say it is true and I understand why that is and you may not.

A timid mind avoids exercise.

5/9/2010 1:33:18 PM –

[Jonah 4:3 Therefore now, O LORD, take, I beseech thee, my life from me; for it is better for me to die than to live.]

The meek find the light just after the end of the rope. As your friends increase your honest observations decrease. Happiness is relative to awareness not pleasure. The main flaw in democracy is that it assumes everyone is equally aware. You have looked deep enough when you wished you wouldn't have looked so deep. Depression suggests awareness hurts. Darkness is not evil as much as it is blindness taking many backward steps in hopes of a forward step. Starting a fire and putting it out is not progression. Wealth is not relative to what you have in your wallet it is relative to what you need in your wallet. A fool may learn from his missteps and understand they were not missteps. Purpose abhors victory. If you live long you may not have lived well. Peace and fear are often indistinguishable. Time cannot be saved it can only be perceived. I am willing to talk about whatever you thought you are talking about.

Perfection is plentiful in the absence of observers. Definitions of words are probabilities mixed in with intense moments of delusion. Reaching the top of the mountain is possible; assisting others to reach it is comical. An empty jug has more value than a full one.

"Because one doesn't like the way things are is no reason to be unjust towards God." Victor Hugo

We have reading , writing and math to make life easier and make life "better" but in teaching it to young children it veils the God image in man, right hemisphere, and the chances a being can ever restore their right hemisphere traits to sound levels fully is slim after the education has veiled them. As a species we are paying an extremely heavy price just because we do not like the way things are. The "world" of the scribes perhaps have no experts that understand the written education hinders the mind and therefore the scribes have no experts that understand what kind of damage is caused to the mind after one applies the remedy and restores their right brain traits to a conscious level after the education has veiled said traits. Perhaps it all comes down to the value of the mind. The mind is intangible and thus may be perceived to have no value on a materialistic scale. Perception cannot be taught but can be altered. The opportunities of tomorrow are the problems of today. There is a core problem and many symptoms. Any decision based on numbers lacks awareness. If the average being understood what was required to be considered a follower of a Jesus they would avoid the topic all together. When failure is looked at as an understanding one stops failing. If you want to be happy close your eyes. If you want to be alive, open your eyes. Compassion tends to be a symptom of fear; compassion for a pit will keep one in it. It is easy to speak about the truth when all the fear is gone. The sinister has an aversion to the light and it must kill the light to protect itself and it sees that as logical and proper.

5/9/2010 1:55:38 PM

5/9/2010 8:41:49 PM –

X = hypothalamus

Y = amygdala

Z = reading, writing, and math

A = mind after one applies remedy

B = sense of time perception dimension

C = sense of now perception dimension

D = remedy

$Z + X = B$

$Z + (X + D) + Y = C$

After the education X is very sensitive. X is sending fight or flight signals over words, pictures, sounds, music and that is abnormal. So X is hyper sensitive and Y is the memory for X. So the remedy is to get X to give its strongest signal and that is relatively easy because X is hyper sensitive. If one is in an old cemetery in broad daylight fifty miles from any help they perhaps will not be afraid at all but at night the hypothalamus may start giving certain death signals, fight or flight signals, but the only factual thing that happened was it became night. This means the hypothalamus is giving

58

fight or flight signals because of visual changes. Some people that sense time may not think the word "ass" is evil or bad but some may think it is and say "That is a bad or evil word so do not say it.", but in reality that persons hypothalamus is giving them the "fight or flight "signal because they were told the word "ass" is bad or evil and were perhaps punished or scolded when they heard that word or said that word and their amygdala remembered that. What this means is a person that gets all that education in turn has a hypersensitive hypothalamus and thus can be easily controlled with fear tactics. "You will go to hell if you say that word "ass"." And some scribes may never say that word again ever because of that simple fear tactic suggestion. "That music is devil music", so some scribes will never listen to that particular sound again and if they hear it they may also say "That music is the devil's music." This is the neurosis and the fear that it breeds is the spirit of fear. It is impossible the sound of a word on its own merits will ever harm anyone unless ones says certain words around lunatics that fear certain words and thus sounds. "If you say that word it proves you have no morals." That is an elementary fear tactic used to manipulate weak minds into doing as they are told with "peer pressure" aspects. "You will not be moralistic like we are if you say that word and that is a tragedy so please never say that word again because we want you do be like we are." The extreme fear caused by the hyper active hypothalamus caused by all the left brain favoring education creates the herd mentality. " He is not one of us because he does not fear the words and sounds and music we fear so he is evil because our group certainly is not evil."

X = a "cuss" word or certain music

Y = potential harm

Z = acceptance

A = fear

B = not liked, hated, out of favor

X + Y + A = Z

This equation is saying "If you want to be accepted you better do as we do." This is not talking about deeds like physically harming people, this is talking about sounds and words which are intangible. These people are not saying you will go to hell if you harm someone they are saying you will go to hell if you make a grunt or listen to a grunt or sound and that logic is on the level of "out of touch with reality" and that is what schizophrenia is.

X = B

If you say X or listen to X you will be hated, out of favor and not liked and that is exactly what a fear tactic is and fear tactics only work on people that have fear and fear is a symptom of all the left brain favoring education. So education appears to be a perfect slave, manipulation, perception altering invention but the complexity is, the scribes do not even know that because if they did they would not give it to their own children or at least if they did they would assist their own children with the remedy afterwards. This suggests the only logical conclusion is mentally hindered people (scribes) are making decisions that show indications they are mentally hindered. If the education was a conspiracy to make everyone prone to fear and make everyone mentally hindered then the ones in charge of that would ensure no one ever wakes up or negates that mental hindering and it does appear like that relative to suicidal people who are attempting to "defeat their fear of death" or they are "mindful of death" which is the remedy and "society" tries to "cure" them with pills but society (the scribes) do not even know that is what they are doing. This is why the ancient texts speak of beings possessed by the devil and that is the same concept as an insane person; a person that cannot reason. If an adult scribe is going around telling children they will go to hell for saying a word or telling them they will go hell for listening to certain music that adult scribe has to be out of touch with reality if they seriously believe that. If a person is in a dark room after watching a scary movie and their mind says "Turn on the lights or a spook will harm you" and that person does, they are reacting to hallucinations caused by their hyperactive hypothalamus. Since one is always a slave to their perception there are no pills that will make their perception stop telling them words or sounds or shadows are going to harm them and thus the only solution is to "fix" the perception signals. Since the education causes a mental hindering only an extreme shock on a mental level will fix it. The difference between fear and reasoning is logic. A parent scribe may hit their child for saying a cuss word but that is not a reasoned decision that is a fear based decision. This punishment of a child for saying a cuss word is actually relative to fear, pride and ego on the part of the scribe adult.

If the adult scribe takes the child to a friend's house and that child says a cuss word that will reflect back on the parent scribe and that parent scribe will have their pride, ego harmed and they fear that or are timid about that, so that fear makes them punish their child for saying the cuss word around a friend. The factual reality is a word is a sound and thus intangible so the parent scribe is going through pride, fear, and emotional stress as the result of a sound. So the parent scribe in order to protect their ego and pride will punish their child for saying a cuss word and thus the parent scribe is doing things to protect their pride. That parent scribe perceives they are doing a righteous deed by punishing their child for saying a cuss word but in reality they are acting on the signals from their hyperactive hypothalamus. The school system is considering bring back paddling to schools and I know they paddle children for saying cuss words and they perceive it is completely reasonable to do that. The scribes believe it is proper to hit a child if that child makes a grunt the scribes do not agree is a proper grunt. If a scribe allows their child to say a grunt the other scribes suggest is an improper grunt that initial scribe may be looked at as an outcast , so again the initial scribes actions are based on fear, pride, ego and peer acceptance. This means the only reason a scribe parent punishes their child for saying a cuss word is to be accepted by their peers, other scribes. Just writing that I am certain some scribes will say "He has no morals because he does not think some words and some music is evil so clearly he has no conscience and he is evil." and at the same time they will brag about giving innocent children all that left brain favoring education starting at the age of six means they are righteous for doing so and have no thoughts that it may have some bad side effects on the child considering the child's mind does not even develop until the child is well into their twenties. Sometimes a scribe will get very drunk and start cussing and show no fear of words and that is a symptom doing drugs unveils the right hemisphere and the God image in man has no timidity. Right hemisphere sees holistically so it is logical it would not fear any words or have any prejudice to any words or sounds at all. So when right brain is at full power in the conscious state of mind the word "ass" looks the same as the word "grass" and "bass" and "brass" meaning the words have no greater value than each other so there is no prejudice. They can throw you in jail if you say a cuss word around a scribe if that scribe says "He is disturbing the peace with all of his evil words he is saying around my child I love so much." "I have to protect my child from the evil words so throw that being in jail and save us all from him." This spirit of fear is the control method and safety is a fear word. "If you do not throw that being that is cussing in public in jail we will not be safe and the children will not be safe." You can take over the whole world if you can create an argument based on protecting children and the scribes have. "We want to give all the world children our "brand" of education so they will be safe and we will be safe and the world will be safe." The whole premise of the scribes is they just want to help you because clearly you were born mentally ruined because God only makes ruined minds and so all children are born mentally ruined and then the great scribes show up with their God correcting "wisdom " education and now you are better. Your IQ will never exceed 205 and the scribes have made sure of it. You fear words, you fear colors, you fear sound, your fear music you, fear pictures, you fear yourself, you fear what you look like, you fear what others look like. The scribes fixed you well. The scribes have turned you from a genius mentally sound wise being in to a mental joke of all reality and I am the comedian of the universe and you are my material. The ancient texts compared the scribes to snakes, beasts, cattle but

I cannot suggest after that education one is like a snake or a cattle because a snake and a cattle are of sound mind. A cow does not run in terror when it gets dark. A snake does not run in terror when it gets dark. A cow does not cringe when you say a cuss word or show the cow a nude cow picture.

The difficulty level of the remedy is completely relative because after the remedy is applied the remedy does not seem like such a big deal to apply but before one applies the remedy it appears so difficult to apply many simply cannot apply it ever. In principle one simply scares their self greatly and then when in a situation where their mind says "You will die for sure from the darkness or spooks" and then person just says mentally "I don't care" and that is the entire remedy completely. It is done. The effects of applying the remedy will take effect in about thirty days. So the concept of the remedy can be applied in perhaps infinite different ways as long as the hypothalamus believes certain death is going to happen and one ignores that signal when it is given, the remedy always works. I only applied it once, accidentally. Another way to look at it is, I only applied the remedy once and it worked and now I cannot ever apply it again so in that respect I do not have the luxury of a repeat experiment. I cannot repeat applying the remedy simply because the amygdala remembers I applied the remedy and it remembers when my hypothalamus gave me the death signal I said "I don't care". So the remedy is permanent and that is great because one in the neurosis may spend years and years attempting to apply this one second mental exercise but once it is applied it is for life. As long as one understands the concepts of the remedy they can take those concepts and apply it to many variations to achieve the same results. This means the remedy is not set in stone relative to details but the concept is. A simple version of the remedy would be for a scribe to watch a scary movie, maybe read a scary story, turn out the lights, maybe go to the basement with the lights out and it is probable the hypothalamus will give one the death signal. What really makes the remedy so difficult for a scribe to apply is they are trapped by that hyperactive hypothalamus and that means the hypothalamus may be giving near death or potential death signals long before the person gets to a situation that will allow the full measure death signal. For example, If I say, "Go to that spooky abandoned house in the middle of the woods alone at night", the scribes hypothalamus may say "Never do that you will die" and that is not a death signal that is a premature death signal that will scare the scribe from even considering going to that house in the woods at night, alone. So probable death scares the scribes, potential death scares the scribes and even improbable death scares the scribes and in order to apply the remedy properly one has to face certain death but only relative to the scribe's perception. It is an [If then] type of situation. The mind has to be convinced if the person does not seek help or run they will die. There are certainly ways one can "kind of apply" the remedy but that only means they "kind of" return to sound mind. There is a concept about seeing the door as a wall. If one looks at their fear as a wall they are trapped by their fear and if one looks at the fear as a door they have a very large door to walk through. If a scribe is afraid of a dark house in the middle of the woods at night that is good because they can apply the remedy relatively safely. If a scribe is afraid after watching a scary movie that is even better. This is all complex because a person relies on their perception and thus their fight or flight signals to stay safe, but after the education ones fight or flight signals are off the scale so one cannot trust them and that is what "deny yourself " and "fear not" and 'submit" is all about. One might say "I am not afraid of a house in the middle of the woods at night" but the problem is their hypothalamus does not rely on that, it is its own man. For example one might be walking down a path in the woods alone at night towards the spooky abandoned house and then hear a wolf off in the distance howl and their hypothalamus might start giving fight or flight signals and this has nothing to do with the house it has to do with the hypothalamus giving fight or flight signals for just about everything. A person does not tell the hypothalamus when to give fight or flight signals so a person can be totally calm in that spooky house in the woods alone at night and if a strong wind blows outside and a door slams as a result in that house that person may go into cardiac arrest relative to getting fight or flight signals. The thing is, in that extreme left brain state thoughts are very linear and slothful so the fear keeps building up until the person either runs or submits. Once a person runs the fear dissipates and once the person submits the fear dissipates. The only difference between a person that runs when they get the death signal and a person that submits when they get the death signal is a state of mind called meek. If one is arrogant they run and if one is meek they don't run when they get the death signal. This appears very odd or foolish but the reality is, being meek is the only way to tell the amygdala to tell the hypothalamus to stop sending so many false fight or flight signals. You are not suicidal because you submit when your mind tells you a shadow is going to kill you in that dark house alone in the woods, it is just suicidal is what meek is, it's a form of submission so you are

66

not going to die because of a shadow in a house in the middle of the woods but your hypothalamus will tell you that you factually will for sure and so it requires self control to set that hypothalamus straight and that is achieved by ignoring that death signal and the amygdala remembers that. There has never ever been any proof that a ghost or spook has ever killed anyone ever and that is a fact so one can see that is reasonable and probable but the hypothalamus is not hooked up to cognitive ability it is more like a mind of its own. If a person hears the wind blow in that abandoned house in the woods that means the hyperactive hypothalamus is going into action regardless of all reason and logic. Let's look at the details in how Mohammed found God. He mediated in a cave. So a person is sitting there in daylight meditating in a cave and that seems rather uneventful but then it gets dark and that cave is pitch black, that cave is far away from any help, that cave could have anything in it, maybe even spooks and then one can see the meditation is far more effective while potential "action" is a foot. So in daylight the cave meditation is no big deal but at night the cave mediation separates the men from the boys so to speak. This suggests the actual lack of daylight is enough to make the hypothalamus give potential death signals or fight or flight signals on the merits of darkness itself. If one may get a death signal just because the lights are out that is a very abnormally working hypothalamus. In the machine state one can attempt to be afraid but because right brain processes thoughts are in random access a prolonged state of fear is not possible simply because after even a few seconds the thoughts change to something else even if one is afraid. So a scribe may become afraid and then something happens and becomes more afraid and then something happens and they fear for their life in this dark place but when right brain random access is working those kinds of prolonged linear thought processes are not possible. So one can see Mohammed went to that cave to mediate and when it got dark instead of running he submitted and that is all it takes. So some people would be in that cave at night and they would run and that may appear to be logical but the truth is one has to submit in the face of fear and that is not a sign of weakness that is a sign of strength. Anyone can run when their mind says "death is coming" and very few can submit when their mind says "death is coming". It is a mental decision that takes one second and it is done and it will kick in about thirty days later when ones loses their sense of time, an indication right brain paradox has come back to the conscious state, and it takes over a year relative to a calendar to get use to infinity, no sense of time perception dimension. By applying this remedy you are factually going from one perception dimension to the total opposite perception dimension so it is logical it will take you some time to adjust but you are not adjusting to abnormality, you are adjusting to normalcy or consciousness. You are not going to an alternate perception dimension you are returning to the normal perception dimension and so you are going to gain so much, have so many senses added to you such as intuition, complexity, lightning fast processing, you will have to adjust. So the adjustment is only because all of these right brain traits that were veiled by the education are coming back online. Simply put, you are not use to them because they didn't even develop fully until the frontal lobe developed after you were twenty and they were veiled long before that perhaps even after a few years of education. Another way to look at it is after you apply the remedy it is going to take you at least a year to adjust to cerebral abilities you never felt before because you never felt them before; they were veiled before they were even warmed up. So the best candidates for this remedy are the meek which are the depressed and suicidal because they are already mindful of death and looking for a way out of here anyway. If a person is already thinking about literally killing their self they perhaps would not mind going to a spooky place to see if a ghost will kill them, so to speak. So this remedy is not about taking advantage of the depressed it is simply the depressed and suicidal are meek and that is the state of mind one has to be in to apply the remedy the full measure.

[Matthew 5:5 Blessed are the meek: for they shall inherit the earth.]

Blessed are the depressed and suicidal scribes because they are the most valuable relative to applying the fear not remedy. This is a good example of the reverse thing. The scribes think the suicidal and depressed need help but in fact they are far more in touch with reality than the scribes who seek to "fix" them perhaps ever will be.

5/11/2010 7:58:44 AM –

Factitious Disorder - Munchausen Syndrome - Patients with this disorder knowingly fake symptoms, but do so for psychological reasons not for monetary or other discrete objectives as in the case of Malingering. They usually prefer the sick role and may move from hospital to hospital in order to receive care.

This condition is happening in almost all scribes but it comes out as different aspects that are not considered a disorder. For example a scribe may seek to have great wealth and then base their life on the "suffering" they endure to get the money or the suffering they went through to get the money or wealth. They will say 'You don't know what I had to go through to get to where I am at." They are faking symptoms. They tend to be on the surface "happy" but they are very depressed because they find all of their wealth and money does not make them happy but they cannot show that because they dedicated their whole life to making that money and so to admit the money and wealth did not make them happy they would have to admit they wasted their life seeking something that did not make them happy. This factitious disorder is a person that seeks attention and that is a symptom of ego and also a symptom of depression. Some scribes will buy lots of land or lots of material things and that is their form of seeking attention. "Look at me and all the wealth I have, I certainly must be happy and wise." The principle in society is to chase this material monster and that is the race relative to society and that is the purpose and that creates suffering and so there is this common suffering caused by the "race". One cannot really become wealthy unless they are ruthless because everyone else is attempting to become wealthy. This dog eat dog concept simply means one is suffering because they are seeking progression in a system that requires one to take advantage of others to progress. Right hemisphere knows exactly what is going on at all times but when reduced to a subconscious level by the education one is not aware of many things they are doing, they know not what they do. Sometimes a child even as early as age ten or twelve will do something for attention. The attention gained is simply an ego boost and that is of value to a person with pride and that attention gained is relative to satisfaction. So the mind in a scribe is seeking satisfaction because the right hemisphere aspects are veiled and if they were not, satisfaction would not be possible because when right hemisphere is in the conscious state ego and pride are not possible in the machine state or in the now. Think about a celebrity. They will go to the news and say "I had an eating disorder and now I am cured of it and I am a much better person now and everything is fantastic and I am happy." An eating disorder is not possible when a person is of sound mind because the eating disorder is a symptom one is seeking satisfaction from food and then one is seeking attention because they eat so much and then one gets this "everyone feels sorry for me because of my eating disorder" and so that simply encourages the eating disorder because it boosts the scribes ego. This concept applies to drug use, controlling things, abuse to one's self or others and so it all comes down to simply a person faking symptoms to get the pride and ego boost that is achieved through that. A person may get some sort of body modification surgery and then regret it and then seek sympathy and turn it into a suffering aspect just to get attention. There are very few people that get body modification surgery and keeps it to their self. They in fact tell everyone and so the body modification is simply an aspect one accomplishes to boost their ego and pride so the person is actually harming their perfect body in order to get attention. This disorder comes down to a person doing something to get attention because attention boosts ego and pride relative to the amount of attention they seek. This is not because the person is a bad person this is because all that left brain favoring education has turned their pride and ego up so high they are actually doing some very odd things to satisfy that pride and ego. Other words the emotions are the drug and in order to feel the drug one has to do certain things to get attention. One symptom of this disorder is a person has a history of depression and suicidal thoughts. The absolute reality is there are no human beings on this planet that got all the left brain favoring education and didn't apply the remedy to one degree or another that is not depressed. Another way to look at it is an entire hemisphere of their mind is hindered or veiled to a degree so they do not have full mental capacity so they are suffering so they are depressed and it just comes out in so many ways one cannot really determine what they all are. Sometimes a parent will be very controlling and that is a symptom of depression. Sometimes a parent won't be controlling at all and that is a symptom of depression. Some scribes work out and "eat the right foods" to the point of obsession and that is a symptom of depression and that also is a symptom of seeking attention. 'I am suffering because I have to work out every day for five hours and then eat this food I dislike, look at me, look at me and my suffering." A "criminal" will break the law and then suggest how much they are suffering and law enforcement will suggest how much they are suffering attempting to arrest all the "criminals." and both gain attention and thus pride and ego boosts for suggesting they are suffering, but inside their mind they are simply seeking attention. They are faking disorders to gain attention from their peers and when they gain attention from their perceived peers their ego and pride is boosted and they get a nice emotional rush. Contrast that with a hardcore serious suicidal person. They may seem like they are seeking attention and that certainly plays a role because they have the ego and pride seeking also but when it comes down to it they are seeking to die and there is no reward for dying and no emotions to be gained once they are dead so they are not in this attention seeking aspect because mentally they are seriously seeking to check out literally. Of all the mental aspects one can seek to face, death is the greatest of them all so it is logical a person that is suicidal has such a strong mental fortitude they are seeking to master the hardest mental conditioning one can ever accomplish in life. Nothing compares to defeating ones fear of impermanence so the suicidal are often mocked by the "normies" because the suicidal are attempting the hardest thing there is to overcome in all of life and the "normies" are jealous of that subconsciously. Getting a job and making money and seeking attention is all stupidity in contrast to overcoming ones fear of impermanence before one has to so the suicidal are putting this huge burden on their self willingly and this is a symptom they are trying to unveil right hemisphere often unknowingly. "Deny yourself", "Seek the shadow of death and fear not" "Submit" these are huge burdens a suicidal person places on their self and they are not consciously aware that is what they are doing. The suicidal are seeking to deny their self the full measure but they do not see it that way, they see their self as a loser and fool and a failure and that is because they are meek and thus the winners. All the beings with money and material wealth and popularity are the absolute losers and the suicidal and the depressed are the absolute winners among the scribes and although your mind is so mentally destroyed you may not be able to grasp that, it is absolute truth. The ones that have applied the remedy the full measure are nothing or in nothingness mentally so one can call them whatever they want and they will probably agree with it. All of the scribes wish they were winners like the depressed and suicidal scribes and that is why they mock them and handle them with kid gloves because those scribes feel better about their self and they get an ego and pride boost in the presence of the meek. If one fakes a disease or condition and goes to a doctor and the doctor finds out it is a fake that person is going to feel embarrassed and ashamed and those emotions are as good as any when one is addicted to emotions. When ones emotional capacity is off the scale which is what it is when right hemisphere traits are veiled, any emotions will work so the emotions are not as important as the strength of the emotions one achieves. It just so happens the depressed and suicidal are addicted to the "sad" emotions. You can see the wealthy and they have lots of material things and they appear happy and pleased and they are on the surface addicted to the "happy" emotions but inside they are very depressed because they are aware subconsciously of all the people they had to harm to get all that material wealth. A monetary system does not consider people being harmed in its equation and that goes for environmental harm which equates to human suffering and harm. The scribes harm lots of people to get on the fortune 500 list. You would never find Moses, Jesus, Jonah, Mohammed or Buddha on the Fortune 500 because they have cerebral wealth and so as cerebral wealth increases desire for material wealth decreases. If you have cerebral wealth you have wealth and so the material wealth desires fade away. An economic system hates that reality because if everyone had cerebral wealth they would leave the rat race for material wealth. Show me one person on the Fortune 500 that understands what the tree of knowledge is and the remedy to it and the implications of it and you will understand none of them have any wealth they just have paper they rub on their head in their infinite attempts to fill the hole in their mind. The wealthy scribes have so much to let go of just so they can make the one second mental decision that is the remedy it is probable they can never do it and with the depressed they are already pondering letting go so it is probable they can apply the remedy. The scribes have this cut and dry approach to psychology but until they factor in what all that left brain favoring education does to the mind of a child over a prolonged period of time they will never be able to figure psychology out. There are only people who got the education and have not applied the remedy and thus are mentally unsound and exhibit symptoms of that and then there are beings that have applied the remedy and return to sound mind and exhibit symptoms of that and then there are the last vestiges of human beings left on the planet known as tribes that never got the education at all and thus never had to go through the mental destruction caused by the education. If modern society was not a lunatic asylum as Nezchez suggested the very first thing they would do when they discovered written education does hinder the mind when pushed on small children is seek out these tribes and seek their advice on everything. I do not detect the tribes mentally harm their children on an industrial scale starting at the age of six so just the fact modern society seeks advice from modern society shows why we are never going to escape the lunatic asylum. Another way to look at it is [Mark 3:23 ..., How can Satan cast out Satan?]

A lunatic cannot talk a lunatic out of lunacy.

Lunacy: behavior that is regarded as unintelligent, inconsiderate, or misguided, or an example of it.

Is it unintelligent and inconsiderate to push left brain education on a child when it mentally hinders them or is that modern society's definition of wise and intelligent and full of foresight? Modern society does not give a dam about children they only give a dam about money, the numbers. As ones mental capacity decreases one needs artificial means to shore up that deficit. That is why the tribes that live in nature do not have an economic or monetary system because they have no mental deficit.

Deficit: the amount by which a total is less than it should be.

Human beings have this right hemisphere that has traits that are so powerful even beings that have full function of that hemisphere cannot determine how powerful it is and modern society unknowing makes sure that hemisphere is destroyed or turned off all together via laws in all the children starting at the age of six and that is not even considering the third mind aspect.

"What it comes down to is that modern society discriminates against the right hemisphere." - Roger Sperry (1973) Neurobiologist and Nobel Lauriat

If you do not even listen to beings you give your vanity medals to, you perhaps certainly will not listen to me either. As a species we factually cannot function if we continue to hinder right hemisphere so why the hell are you walking around saying words like hope, love, peace, joy and happiness when you perceive the veiling of the complex powerhouse of the mind as a wise decision? I would not tell six billion people to go mindfully kill their self if that was not a wise solution. You can't say you care when you only show symptoms you don't care. You can't say you love when you only show's symptoms you hate. You can't say you are wise when you only show symptoms of stupidity. You can't say you are happy when you only show symptoms of suffering. You can't say you are alive when you are only showing symptoms of death.

"Female Orgasmic Disorder: A disorder which may result from a traumatic experience, but can also be acquired through problems within relationships. There are those for whom the problem is of lifelong duration and for others the problem may present in generalized settings or be specific to situational settings."

[A disorder which may result from a traumatic experience] Firstly traumatic is relative. Traumatic experiences are relative to ones mental capacity to comprehend events they experience. This disorder is really just a female scribe that is a nervous wreck and this disorder applies to male scribes also and they are a nervous wreck because their right brain random access thought patterns no longer factor into their conscious thoughts. The scenario is when this being reaches a point of having sex these "traumatic" thoughts are recalled and the emotions and time stamps are attached and so this creates nervousness and so this sexual dysfunction is relative to the dysfunction in their thoughts. This disorder is not relative to having some physical flaws it is all in their "head" so to speak and that means it is relative to their thoughts. Another way to look at it is if this being had right brain aspects unveiled they would not be effected by traumatic events to begin with and thus they would not be nervous to begin with because both of those thought aspects are relative to only having linear slothful thoughts and that is not possible at all with right brain traits unveiled and factoring into the conscious state fully. One cannot exhibit mental symptoms one is unable to exhibit is one way to look at it. The traumatic event aspect is really a symptom the right hemisphere is hindered or not factoring into one conscious thought patterns. I bring up the police scribes and the soldier scribes because they are extreme examples or they are the extreme results of having right hemisphere veiled. They suffer the most or show the most profound symptoms of traumatic experiences. The police and the soldiers tend to literally end up dying or killing their self because of the traumatic experiences they encounter. Think about a war situation and think about a soldier watching this traumatic event and then think about a rabbit next to that soldier watching the same event. That soldier may start to show mental distress because they witnessed that traumatic event but that rabbit would not. Let's say the soldier watched a house get blown up from a distance he knew the "enemy " was in and the rabbit saw that also. The problem is not the "traumatic" event, the problem it is how the observer of the traumatic event mentally processes that observation. How that traumatic event is stored in the mind is what creates the problem. A lion kills large animals for food and he does it by biting them and that creates quite a bit of blood and usually the lion is covered in blood after a kill but that lion does not have PTSD yet that event is perhaps more traumatic than what a soldier or police officer would experience on a daily basis average. When right brain traits are veiled observations of events are stored with time stamps and emotions and when right brain traits are not veiled then events are stored as concepts and no concept is stronger than any other concept. When the sense of time is greatly increased, emotions and emotional capacity is greatly increased and greatly prolonged one is going to have a host a symptom's as a result of that. A soldier is haunted by the memory of a traumatic event and that goes the same with police officers and because their right brain aspects are veiled those events keep playing over and over until the being cannot stand it any longer. There is no way to stop PTSD until right brain traits are restored. People with PTSD end up trying to take drugs, drink and a host of other thing just to forget the traumatic event but they cannot change how it is recorded so they tend to self destruct attempting to forget this traumatic event. They drink to forget but it never changes their perception of the "traumatic" event and that is suffering. When right brain is restored the memory is very complex but one is like an absent minded professor and their thoughts are random access and those thoughts do not have time stamps and do not have emotions attached. When one has no sense of time a traumatic event that happen yesterday may seem like it happened life times ago and that is along the lines of the quick and the dead. For example a person mentally gets over traumatic events so fast because they have no sense of time and their memory does not record time nor emotions. The scribes will suggest emotions are good and then when people start killing their self because of the emotions the same scribes will say "Take our pills, emotions are bad."

Deficit: the amount by which a total is less than it should be.

When the mind is less than it should be the being cannot function. One cannot veil or hinder right hemisphere even one percent or the being is doomed and the education veils right hemisphere to a subconscious state completely so there is no hope unless one restores that aspect and if one does not the show is over. If a person experiences a traumatic event and they are not over that traumatic experience by the end of the day it is only because their thought processes have been reduced to sloth because right brain aspects are veiled. If two cars got in an accident outside my house and bodies were thrown everywhere and blood was everywhere and people were screaming and death was in the air I could observe that and within an hour it would seem like it happened a lifetime ago and even when I recall it, it would be like a concept but no time stamps and no emotions and it would have no more weight in my thoughts than a picture of the ocean. That has to do with one thing only. Right hemisphere has no prejudice; is holistic. That does not mean I am immune to detecting suffering it simply means I do not have a nervous breakdown when I observe suffering. When milk spills it is recorded in the mind as an observation and not as a traumatic experience. A scientist running an experiment is not emotional and nervous he is actually observing and detecting patterns and one cannot do that if they are emotional, very well. This is relative to the concept about do not take it personal. Getting all "caught" up mindfully in an event means one is no longer and observer of the event. One cannot be an observer and also be caught up in the event because if one is caught up in the event they have a conflict of interest in the event and therefore their observations are tainted. It is far more healthy to be indifferent to what one observes than to be emotional about everything one observes. Outside of actual physiological damage all of these psychological disorders go back to one core problem, the education veils right brain aspects and then relative to a pharmaceutical companies perception, society becomes a cash cow. Even nervousness by itself causes so much physiological damage and takes its toll on people and nervousness is caused by a thought that is retained in the thought processes. In the machine state or the now, nervousness is simply not possible because it is time relative. Another way to look at it is as long as the thoughts are random access then one factually cannot stress out about any one thought. What that means is the scribes have right brain traits veiled and so relative to their thought processes they are compulsive.

Compulsive: exerting a powerful attraction or interest.

The scribes cannot get thoughts to change so they fester in their mind for a lifetime and they never leave, hardly change and so their thoughts are like a pool instead of a stream. The scribes have a powerful attraction to certain thoughts and they cannot let go of them but not because they are stupid but because their right brain random access aspect is at a subconscious level. One cannot be compulsive about anything if their thoughts are changing on a second to second basis relative to a clock in absolute random access order. Relative to your perception I am compulsive about writing books but relative to my perception I don't even recall exactly what I have written so my mind does not even register I have even written one book. I look at each book as a chapter and my book has infinite chapters so I will never even write one book and so it is not a compulsion. I don't even recall what I wrote a thousand words ago let alone what I wrote yesterday let alone what I wrote a month ago and so if I read what I wrote a month ago I would read it and say "That is pretty interesting but I better clarify it in my book." I do recall the concepts well though just not the details. I can't get tired writing because tired is a symptom one's mind registers time. This machine state of mind is exactly why the scribes took advantage of the "tribes". The tribes did not really see being a slave was that big of a deal. If the tribes would have seen being a slave was that big of a deal they probably would have run. The tribes were of sound mind and saw holistically and being a slave is not different than being free because free and slave are label's and suggest prejudice. This is why the scribes have taken over everything because the ones of sound mind see holistically and have no prejudice. I have to fight with all of my might to judge the scribes because my natural tendency in this holistic state of mind is to see the mental hindering of children as beauty just like I would see not mentally hindering children as beauty. It is a very simple concept.

Q = sound mind

R = extreme left brain state

X = holistic perception

Y = seeing parts or prejudice perception

Z = aversion

A = indifference

Q + X = A : R +Y = Z

Harmony or a holistic perception seeks harmony or has no prejudice. Disharmony or seeing parts perception seeks prejudice. Holistic sounds like I am some spiritual advisor to the stars, it really is just absence of prejudice or one is a poor judge relative to perception. I think a lot of music I didn't care for before the accident sounds just swell now. Clearly I am a poor judge. I think everyone looks perfect. Clearly I am a poor judge. I sometimes think I can convince the species written education taught to young children does harm their mind so clearly I am cursed with poor judgment. In infinity one tends to take on challenges that are infinite.

[Jonah 4:3 Therefore now, O LORD, take, I beseech thee, my life from me; for it is better for me to die than to live.]

Jonah knew there was no way to stop the curse caused by written education thousands of years ago. Jonah knew when to quit. If one gets any spirit from the book of Jonah it is the spirit of knowing when to quit. Knowing when impossibility is reality is the story of Jonah. I did not throw myself in the sea willingly in the middle of a storm from a perfectly floating boat, but Jonah did so I may not ever reach the kind of clarity he reached. Jonah explained exactly how he applied the remedy and not only that he was aware after he initially applied the remedy he had to go and apply it the full measure or try again because he still had fear. What is interesting about that perhaps is he had no teacher or he had no direction relative to contact with other humans so he was a lone wolf. The book of Jonah is clear proof the ancient texts are simply testimonies from various human beings over the course of thousands of years attached to the one collective text. Jonah did not need a following. Jonah did not need friends. Jonah did not need an advisor. Jonah did not need anything from anyone relative to anything. That is an indication of the level of mental clarity Jonah reached by tossing himself into the sea in the middle of a storm from a non sinking boat. If all the ancient texts were reduced to just the book of Jonah there would be nothing lacking. Mohammed wrote about Jonah and he perhaps knew that also. It is along the lines of the concept the truly wise do not seek or need attention. The aspect of the fish in the book of Jonah is the least important aspect in that book yet that is the only aspect the scribes consider. Jonah and the whale is nothing in contrast to what Jonah concluded at the end of the text.

[Jonah 4:11 And should not I spare Nineveh, that great city, wherein are more than sixscore thousand persons that cannot discern between their right hand and their left hand; and also much cattle?]

This question he ended on means there is no solution to the curse.

X = state of mind after one gets the education as a child

Y = the remedy

Z = probability of applying the remedy

X + Y = Z

(Z) = nil

Nil = Jonah 4:11

Nil: nothing or zero.

I look at that as a blessing because I cannot possibly be stressed out or nervous when I am fully aware the probability is zero relative to stopping this curse on the species. Another way to look at it is I write exactly what is on my mind because I am fully aware of the outcome. Happiness is achieved when the mind can comprehend any situation that arises. Since I applied the remedy by accident it means as a species we need to have six billion seven hundred million accidents swiftly and the probability of that is nil. By the time six billion seven hundred million people apply the remedy perhaps six billion seven hundred million children will be taught the education and need to apply the remedy. There are not exactly herds of people that have applied the remedy running around in this narrow and it has nothing to do with morals it is an indication of how devastating the mental damage is, caused by the education.

[Mark 3:26 And if Satan rise up against himself, and be divided, he cannot stand, but hath an end.]

"What it comes down to is that modern society discriminates against the right hemisphere." - Roger Sperry (1973) Neurobiologist and Nobel Lauriat]

Let's substitute Satan for modern society, the scribes. Modern society discriminates against right hemisphere with the education technology and in turn has a mind divided and as a group they are in turn divided as a result of the left brain seeing parts prejudice because the education technology favors left hemisphere.

[And if [modern society] rise up against himself, and be divided(left brain seeing parts way too much), he cannot stand, but hath an end.]

This comment in Mark is simply saying in spirit "You cannot be serious if you think as a species you can hinder or turn off an entire hemisphere of the mind and survive." This comment in Mark is saying in spirit "The scribes have no future but death if they continue to discriminate against right hemisphere, period." There is no power in this universe that can cancel out the fact civilization discriminates against an entire hemisphere of the mind to the degree it veils it and silences it all together. There is no supernatural that can make up for that stupidity. Do you think supernatural is going to come down here and unveil everyone's right hemisphere because I do not see that happening at all. What on earth raised you and gave you the impression discriminating against right hemisphere via the "wisdom education" is going to lead to anything but death for the species? I would like to know who your teacher is that told you discriminating against right hemisphere is a wise decision and if you teacher did not tell you the education does discriminate against right hemisphere in a major way it means they are out of touch with reality so your teacher is a schizophrenic lunatic. You can take all your money and cram it down your throat and see if that will assist you to defeat your fear of death and then you can suggest money has value and if that does not assist you in defeating your fear of death mindfully it may assist you in defeating your fear of death literally and then you can come back from the second death and suggest money does have value. You think there is hope. You want there to be hope because subconsciously you are fully aware there is no hope.

Hope: a feeling that something desirable is likely to happen.

Thousands of years ago Jonah wrote this as his final comment on the entire situation relative to what the tree of knowledge has done to us as a species.

[Jonah 4:11 And should not I spare Nineveh, that great city, wherein are more than sixscore thousand persons that cannot discern between their right hand and their left hand; and also much cattle?]

You and all your scribe experts will never ever top his observation. Your ignorance is your hope. As long as you are blind you have hope and the moment you take off the blinders the hope fades away.

"All ye who enter here abandon all hope."

You will never apply the deny yourself remedy until you mindfully abandon all hope. The only beings in this narrow that have hope are the scribes who are absolutely suicidal because they have abandoned all hope. Do you see how flawed your stupid language based on absolutes is now? The only beings that have a chance to restore their minds are the scribes that have no hope. That is the mental state one has to achieve to undo the mental damage the education causes on the mind of a being whose mind does not even develop until they are twenty five. The fact you have a law that says everyone has to get the education technology starting at the age of seven proves you have no cognitive ability at all. Breathing does not prove you have cognitive ability because that is an involuntary trait. You are not showing any symptoms of being alive except for breathing and that is involuntary. Your hope, your ignorance and your fear is a weapon to be used against you. You are fighting and fighting but you do not know why. You are fighting for the children so you can harm them because the scribes bent your mind backwards so when you say love you mean hate. If you at least went on television and said: "Because the children are the future and because we hate the future and thus hate the children we want them all to get the best of our brand of wisdom education possible." I would at least be able to say "The scribes have cognitive ability." A scribe only has one decision in life relative to children and they always pick harm them and for five thousand years they have voted to harm the children. There is not one single country in this narrow that says "Maybe there are problems with all that left brain education considering the child's frontal lobe and thus cognitive ability does not develop until they are twenty five even though beings we gave Nobel Prizes to said it does." Hope is not likely so I ponder why you have so much of it. Do you hope to keep breathing so you can harm more children or so you can watch the ones you have harmed suffer? Do you eat food so you can watch the children you have harmed suffer? You want to continue in the place you are at but you do not know the place you are at. You just want to stay where you are at yet you have no idea where you are at. Mindfully you want to stay where you are at but you do not know where you are at, only I know where you are at because I escaped the place where you are at. Wherever you are at I am not among you. I deny you because you deny me.

You are not what society says you are you are what society is.

5/11/2010 8:42:08 PM – I saw the compulsion caused by seeing parts or by seeing good and evil. One has to purge their emotions and achieve the machine state because the suffering one will notice after they apply the remedy is too much for an emotional human being to bare. I saw a person sweeping their driveway but I did not notice enough dirt to even bother sweeping but I could read the person and they just wanted all the dirt to go away. I could not see the dirt they saw but I could tell they could not stand it. They spend their life sweeping the dirt off of their driveway as the wind blows more back onto the driveway. They see their aversions as progression when it is really compulsion. I must mow the grass so they do not detect I do not have their compulsion. Anyone without their compulsion will not be tolerated. Our shelters are cages to protect us from the dirt we have an aversion to. The education has given us an aversion to the earth. We cannot tolerate anyone that can tolerate earth.

May 12, 2010 (7:44am) -

Religion: the belief in and worship of a superhuman controlling power, especially a personal God or gods.

The god image in man is right hemisphere and the scribes make sure everyone gets that turned off using their "wisdom" education so if one believes in God in this narrow they have to apply the remedy to restore the God image traits in their mind and thus spirit. The problem with that is one has to firstly understand the written education does in fact favor left hemisphere to such a degree is disfavors right hemisphere and thus veils it because the mind is not developed at the age of six or seven when the education starts. So if one loves God that means they are willing to attempt to apply the remedy because it is understood the god image in man is veiled by the education all across the board in this narrow. It is not probable a person could get to the stage of being able to read, write or use math proficiently and not have right hemisphere veiled. Some people have it veiled more than others depending on how proficient they are at the left hemisphere favoring education but the point is if right hemisphere is veiled at all one has to apply the remedy to restore it fully. If right hemisphere traits are veiled one degree that means ones perception is hindered and thus ones cognitive ability is hindered and thus one's mind is hindered. The Native Americans sold much of their land that was not taken from them for very little money because they saw holistically and thus "numbers" are strange and it is hard to judge value in numbers. So they bartered because an item is an item, so one can see value in that tool or item but a number is not so much value relative to a tool. Religion is not about improving it is about restoring what one was before the education so it is a task just to get back to zero. The belief system in religion is not the belief in supernatural. The belief system in religion is that the tree of knowledge, reading, writing and math hinders the mind and thus the spirit. One has to get to that stage of understanding before they will even consider the remedy. So religion is just two doctrines. The first doctrine is written education hinders the mind and thus the spirit and the second doctrine is the remedy restores the mind and thus the spirit and once it is applied one becomes a spokesperson for the religious doctrine because once their mind is restored they are a witness that can explain in detail why the two doctrines are valid and true and fact.

Belief system is not an explanation of religion.

Belief: a feeling that something exists or is true, especially one without proof.

It is not a feeling that all that left brain education hinders the mind considering the cognitive ability does not develop until one is twenty five relative to the frontal lobe. That is not an opinion and is not a belief it is a fact and thus an understanding. So religion is not a belief system it is a fact system. A fact can be proven over and over and shown to be true.

Fact: a thing that is indisputably the case.

One cannot dispute the remedy because any human being that got the education that applies the remedy will negate the effects caused by the education because remedy itself is universal in principle. One will apply

90

the remedy the full measure and come to the conclusion they negated the damage caused by the written education taught to them as a child. That is universal. I am a "spoiler alert". I just tell you everything you will understand after the remedy is applied so if you don't apply the remedy it is still possible I will wake you up just by telling you everything. The complexity is one has to apply the remedy the full measure because only then can one restore their cognitive ability fully. Simply put after one applies the remedy the full measure they will in short order reverse engineer what happened and understand the education is what hindered them mentally. I am not the only human being on the planet that applied the remedy and found out what the tree of knowledge is, I am perhaps just the only human being on the planet that sees no point in not explaining exactly what the tree of knowledge is and its implications and its remedy. I am making a public service announcement. I do not see any reason to be afraid of making a public service announcement. I am mindful many may doubt what I suggest but if they apply the remedy the full measure they factually will not have any argument with what I suggest relative to the damaged caused by the education. The only beings that will not be pleased with what I suggest are beings that cannot suspend their disbelief long enough to apply the remedy. Look at written language and math as very complex inventions that required very intelligent beings to invent and because of the inventions complexity the probability that the inventions would have complex unintended consequences is great. We invented the wheel but that was not very complex so the probability for the wheel having complex unintended consequences was rather slim. The conspiracy theory does not pan out because it is not logical human beings would intentionally invent a tool that made them stupid and thus make life harder. Another way to look at it is an invention is not a tool if it makes things harder. Complex unintended consequences would relate to the side effects of learning the written education and math tools were very subtle. One starts school at the age of seven and by the time they are twelve or fourteen the unintended side effects are complete so over that span of time the effects are very subtle and combined with the fact the child's mind is very delicate it can be shaped very easily by all the left brain favoring aspects of the invention and by other scribes. It does not look like supernatural is going to get us as a species out of this problem because supernatural did not get us into this problem. One can just accept mankind invented something and it had unintended consequences and it just so happens to be written language and math. It has never been about you have to apply the remedy because it is quite an ordeal, the point has always been society does not give a child a choice as to whether the child wants their right hemisphere veiled. Of course because modern society has its right hemisphere veiled it does not have the proper cognitive ability to understand it is not giving a child a choice. Modern society does not believe all the left brain favoring education could possibly ever do any harm to a child's mental development and that can only be an indication of a hindered cognitive ability. If one pushes that left brain favoring tool on a child considering the child's mind does not develop until they are twenty five there factually has to be some devastating consequences but modern society factually perceives there is nothing wrong at all with that scenario and that means modern society is out of touch with reality. I am not picking on one country I am picking on all of them. No country has the right to mentally harm innocent children so now all countries have infinite issues with me. That means all scribes in all countries have infinite issues with me. My purpose is to stop you from harming children no matter what. I don't detect any scribes were concerned about hindering my mind as a child and thus I am not concerned about shattering their perception world. I will remind the scribes when I am concerned about their attempts at laws. The scribes laws suggest an adult must mentally hinder their own child by way of the education and that indicates the laws of the scribes are not be taken seriously because they know not what they do and thus are no longer in touch with reality at all. The scribes have a law that says you have to mentally hinder your own child, compulsory attendance law, and so all their laws after that one are negotiable.

Negotiable : open to discussion or modification. 2 able to be traversed; passable.

As a species we are going to sort this written education and math situation out and we are not going to allow laws to get in the way and that is the law. I refuse to listen to what a scribe suggests relative to this matter because said scribes do not even have the cognitive ability to understand written education factually mentally harms children so they are not at the level mentally to even be in the discussion. The adults are speaking now and the mentally hindered scribes are going to have to adjust to that. There is not going to be a discussion. We have discussed it for five thousand years and now we are going to sort it. We have moved on from discussion to sorting. We are not waiting to see what the scribe experts say. We are not hesitating to see what the popular opinion says. We are not taking any votes, we are simply sorting now.

Sorting : arrange systematically in groups.

Little wheat much chaff.

May 13, 2010 (6:30am) - There is a being from India, an old man, and he suggests he does not need to eat food or drink liquid but only meditate to get energy. The doctors observed him for a week or so with cameras and noted he never went to the bathroom and never ate or drank. This is perhaps interesting because it does appear closing your eyes does give one some sort of energy boost. For example Edison was known to only take cat naps. The logic is, Edison was a very prolific inventor yet he didn't sleep very much and it would seem that the more creative one is the more sleep would be required. For example it takes a lot of brain power to be creative and it takes a lot of brain power to stay in a state of concentration which is what is required to be creative so it would seem one would need lots of sleep to achieve that level of concentration but it appears to be the reverse. This complicates things because if when one is in this no sense of time perception dimension they can achieve some sort of regenerative power just by closing their eyes then it would mean eating and drinking are perhaps "bad habits" at least partially. Another way to look at it is I do not have hunger, yet I eat and drink out of habit perhaps. One thing that does not add up about that is the tribes that never got education and math do eat and do drink. The big question is how much do they eat and drink? There should be complete studies on the tribes that never got the writing education and math because the only way to get a good contrast between the scribes and the tribes is to compare traits or habits each have. For example we know the scribes like to eat three times a day and need about 8 liters of water day but that is assumed to be an absolute but until there is a comparison between the tribes that never got the education and math it will remain just a vague statistic. The scribes have determined the tribes are "stupid" or "dumb" or "misguided" so they do not compare their self to them on an equal scale. Other words the tribes must be stupid because they do not have written language and math and that is an assumption that has no grounds in reality. The tribes should be totally different relative to how they go about things because they are in a completely different perception dimension because they did not get all the left brain favoring education as children. For example a full blown alcoholic looks at a person that does not drink at all differently and a person that does not drink at all looks at a full blown alcoholic differently. Someone who is always on some form of drug looks at someone who isn't differently because their state of consciousness is different. Same principle applies to a person that got education and applied the remedy in contrast to a person that got education and did not apply the remedy. Only one of those two can be in the correct perception dimension. It is not probable it can be normal to have a pronounced sense of time, pronounced sense of hunger and a prolonged emotional capacity and at the same time be normal to have no sense of time and no sense of hunger and no prolonged emotional capacity and this means one of the two is in an altered and abnormal perception dimension and since cognitive ability is relative to perception one of the two in turn also must have an abnormal cognitive ability. Do the tribes that have never been exposed to written education and math and have never been exposed to the scribes or society have overpopulation problems? Do said tribes have environmental problems? Do said tribes have depression problems? Do said tribes have drug abuse problems? The complexity here is they cannot have any contact with the scribes or society in any way because that is the only way to ensure the tribes characteristics are not influenced. For example the Native Americans did not have alcohol and did not have many diseases but then they came into contact with the scribes , society, and then they started having drug problems and starting catching many diseases but the characteristics of the Native Americans did not catch on with the scribes. For example the scribes did not starting living in harmony with nature when they meet the Native Americans. This is a classic example of disharmony seeks disharmony and harmony seeks harmony. The Native Americans adapted to what was on their plate so to speak and the scribes, society did not. The nature of harmony is the ability to adapt and the nature of disharmony is the inability to adapt. This ideal is actually along the lines of the concept "When in Rome." A small child will adapt or be influenced by anything in their environment and that is a symptom of harmony or the ability to mimic and this principle applies to what the Native Americans did, they mimicked the scribes but the scribes did not mimic the Native Americans. The scribes ways were "set in stone". Something along the lines of "I know my ways are right and your ways are different than my ways so your ways are wrong." There is a grey area in all of this because a scribe that applies the remedy has contrast and so they are not easily affected by this mimic aspect any longer, it is along the lines of they have learned their lesson. Another way to look at it is one in the now or the machine state can assume the identity of anything because they are in nothingness which means they can adapt to anything and thus assume the identity of anything and this is apparent when ones looks at some of the traits of say Plato and Mohammed also. They were well versed in many fields. Relative to their perception perhaps they were simply able to adapt and master many fields. Being in the machine state gives one the ability to adapt and thus learn very fast. I am not a psychologist, neurologist, spiritualist, sociologist, or poet or any of those things relative to my perception because I see all of those things as one thing and that one thing is not any of those labels , the correct label is I adapt and learn very fast because I am in the machine state. In order to adapt and learn very fast one has to be able to make mistakes and not be harmed by mistakes or not be frustrated by mistakes or false assumptions because that hinders adaptation. Adaptation has a lot more to do with experimentation and a lot less to do with "getting it right all the time." Getting it wrong so to speak sometime helps one learn more than getting it right and so that means one can potentially learn fastest when they make many mistakes or make many false assumptions but society frowns on that. For example civil law itself is based on someone making a mistake and someone else suffering for it and so that initial person must compensate that secondary person for the mistake. In society a person is idolized for never making mistakes and it is a reason for a national holiday if a person admits to a mistake. I am aware I make many grammar mistakes in the texts but I do not answer to anyone so those grammar mistakes do not even register as anything of importance. You can go read almost any other book and you will find that author perhaps has many people proof read that text and find perhaps not one single misplaced character which shows the author is very self conscious about appearing stupid if they have a grammatical error and that is a symptom of pride and ego considerations based on the assumption if one cannot write "properly" they must not be intelligent. No matter how many grammatical "errors" I make I do not feel stupid so I factually cannot be stupid and that has a lot to do with right brain when at full power in the conscious state is a poor judge and has trouble with labels or maybe I just don't care. Right hemisphere is very philosophical and that is very healthy relative to psychological state of mind. One can seek to be perfect or one can see perfection in things and then they do not have to seek it and that ability is relative to perception.

X = seeing parts 80% of the time and seeing perfection 20% of the time
Y = Seeing perfection 80% of the time and seeing parts 20% of the time

So X is a scribe's perception and after one applies the remedy and unveils right brain traits their perception is Y. This indicates how much right brain factors into perception when it is at 50% or in mental harmony with left brain aspects in the conscious state. Perfection perhaps is not the best word to use because it denotes an absolute so indifferent would be a better word perhaps or lack of aversions. This holistic aspect simply means one sees many more things as proper then they do as improper and with the right brain holistic aspects veiled one sees more things as improper then they see as proper. One has less aversions to what they observe with right brain traits unveiled. Another way to look at it is the remedy does not silence your left hemisphere it simply makes its aspect factor in properly to ones perception. I was reading the ACLU was raising an issue with the police because they found out 700 tickets were written on the basis the person said a cuss word. The interesting thing about laws or getting tickets is they are supposed to assist you to learn but when money is attached to the ticket and thus the learning it crosses a line of a business and then learning becomes secondary and then on another hand laws are really just ways to control people's behavior and often it has nothing to do with morals or proper behavior. I am certain although I am just sitting in my isolation chamber writing down thoughts as they come to mind some scribe will eventually determine I am breaking the law and attempt to "help" me with behavior modification "tickets". The scribes sell many products and they fall under the lines of "Saves you time", "Saves you money", "Makes life easier" but the products rarely do those things or not to the degree they suggest. Life isn't a judgment call.   Sometimes it is best to not save time and not save money. Is a person saving time to save money or saving money to save time? One might suggest there is a lot of saving going on in this narrow and saving is often a nice way of saying control. If you want to help me that means you want to control me. If you want to save me that means you want to control me. To each his own means everyone has their own observations they are acting on or everyone has their own perceptions they are acting on. Since everyone acts on their own separate perceptions the only way to control a person is to alter what they perceive or alter their perception. If one starts off in life with a perception like this : Y = Seeing perfection 80% of the time and seeing parts 20% of the time, and then the years of left brain favoring education changes ones perception to this : X = seeing parts 80% of the time and seeing perfection 20% of the time, one has achieved behavior modification and thus control over that persons perception and thus one has effectively controlled how that person reacts to what they perceive and that is what tyranny over the mind is. Tyranny over the mind means you alter someone's perception on an absolute scale and thus control said beings behavior on an absolute scale.

Einstein suggested the speed of light was the only constant and so that means time is relative and motion is relative. Light travels 299,792,458 metres per second and in the US it is spelled meters. Apparently someone has grammar issues. 899,377,374 feet per second. In physics the speed of light is known as the variable c. Since the speed of light is constant or is the same everywhere unlike motion and time then the speed of light or [c] could be given the number zero on a scale of everything. Other words nothing is faster than the speed of light so all speed would be a negative number in contrast to the constant speed of light which is given the number zero.

Speed of sound is 343 meters per second or 1125 feet per second of course that number is not an absolute in fact there are many different assumptions about the exact speed of sound and this is because it all depends where you are measuring the speed of sound so the speed of sound is relative. So Einstein was suggesting nothing is certain but the speed of light and everything changed relatively speaking around the speed of light and this caused him lots of trouble because it meant essentially everything is just probable. Einstein has a comment where he said essentially "God does not throw dice." because that is what probability means. It is probable when you take a step forward you will take a step forward but it is possible in taking that step you will end up a million light years away from earth. This suggests there is not really any way to know anything on an absolute scale and even the speed of light may simply be probable. So quantum mechanics suggests everything on a subatomic level and on that level there is probability and then when one leaves that level and comes to the atomic level there are absolutes but in reality there are perhaps no absolutes and that is why Einstein attempted for the last part of his life to disprove that reality. Einstein suggested relativity and then he realized what that meant and he spend the rest of life attempting to disprove it and he never did. Einstein attempted to make probability not work but probability is what relativity is. If there was just probability and thus relativity then there is only chaos and Einstein in saying "God does not throw the dice" was suggesting God would not create chaos yet chaos can suggest complexity and paradox and that is a right brain trait. So perhaps Einstein was saying "God must be very complex if this universe appears to be chaos yet still functions in harmony."Another way to look at it is in a true vacuum all one has is probability and that probability is simply illusions or perceptions. This is relative to what happens when a person has their perception altered. If it is all just probability but a person has their perception altered to see absolutes they are going to have trouble. If a person perceives something is factually evil when in reality it is just probably evil their actions and deeds will be completely different. If a person perceives money is required to live and another person perceives money probably is required to live the deeds and actions of those two people will not be identical relative to making money. Simply put a person that has less value on money may not harm others or harm the environment for money and the person that sees money of great value probably will.

This is relative to a perception that sees probability and a perception that sees absolutes.

Constant: remaining the same.

Probable: likely to happen or be the case.

It is likely the speed of light is constant which means it is possible it is not and that is the only proper way to look at it in chaos or a true vacuum. Another way to look at it is the speed of light is a dimensional physical constant but not a perceptional dimensional constant. Other words light takes about 8 minutes to reach earth from the sun but mentally one can imagine light reaching the earth from the sun in less than one second. Before a person takes a step they imagine taking a step. Before a person drives to work they imagine driving to work. Another way to look at it is a person thinks and then they do but one must consider probability in that concept. Modern society is working very hard to talk itself into probability and that is conflicting with control because control is based on absolutes. Freedom is probability which means whatever you do is probably proper and a control structure cannot allow that because control itself suggests dictation of behavior. Every time the physics community says "We know this is a fact" they have to follow it up with "probably." Since the physics community is talking their self into probability it means they probably are not discovering anything at all relative to facts. It is like taking a glass of water and suggesting the glass is full and then the next day one fits another drop into the glass and then suggests: "Yesterday the glass was not really full like I said, but today it is absolutely full." and that cycle keeps repeating and that means nothing is ever certain only probable. It is probable I am writing books and it is possible I am not and that is a fact probably and that is what chaos is and chaos is what illusion is, and illusion is what probability is. This all comes back to perception which means what you perceive is what is because everything centers around the observer, probably. If you hear a cuss word and you feel bad or feel harmed or feel strange then it is probable your perception is unsound. A word is a mild sound and if one reacts to that mild sound on the sound merits alone that is abnormal. If you go into the bathroom and look in the mirror and say three syllable cuss words over and over eventually the cuss word will change its form and you will start to hear other sounds in the cuss words and eventually you will no longer recognize the cuss words. Even if you say the word "Umbrella" over and over swiftly you will start to lose the meaning or the form of "Umbrella" and hear other sounds that may not even be words but you will start to lose the word "umbrella" so to speak. That word will bleed or blend and become other sounds and one will slowly forget about the word umbrella. Words are based on absolutes so in chaos or probability there is going to be problems. Even the word probable is an absolute.

Probable: likely to happen or be the case.

Probable is an absolute expression that something is likely to happen or is the case probably.

Perhaps: expressing uncertainty or possibility.

Perhaps is an absolute expression of uncertainly or possibility, probably.

uncertainly: not known, reliable, or definite.

Uncertainly is an absolutely not known, reliable or definite, probably.

Complexity suggests probability and not absolutes. Linear simple logic suggests absolutes. Right brain deals with complexity so it is logical right brain would like the word perhaps because perhaps suggest probability. Left brain likes simple linear aspects so it is logical left brain would not like the word "perhaps" because "perhaps" suggests probability. What is interesting perhaps is right brain also deals with paradox and paradox suggests complexity so these two aspects may not be two separate aspects but one aspect given two labels. After you apply the remedy you will lose your sense of time and this may be perceived to be the result of the paradox aspect of right hemisphere once again factoring into your perception but this may also be the complexity aspect of right hemisphere factoring into your perception. Deeper still losing your sense of time may be the creative aspect of right hemisphere factoring into your perception. Creativity is relative to imagination or thinking out of the box so it is possible imagination will not allow one to imagine time is passing. The point is perhaps, once perception is altered, everything is altered, perhaps. Simply put the education alters a person's perception probably for life in the majority of cases so it could not do more damage than it does yet there is not even a single suggestion in law or morals or rules that it does anything like that at all.

"Among "other things" I prefer to quote my "self"." It is not probable I am intelligent as much as it is probable my perception is at level that very obvious cause and effect relationships relative to education are apparent. Another way to look at it is if my pattern detection is just normal and that is enough to allow me to detect the education has very probable and obvious potential mental side effects then the whole of society, mainly the control structure of society, the scribes, have perhaps very limited or greatly hindered pattern detection relative to their perception. If one compares my pattern detection to society, the scribes, I appear intelligent or an above average observer but if you compare my pattern detection to normal pattern detection I am average. If one looks at psychology they can see psychology is studying all these behavioral patterns and attempting to control them or understand them and this appears perhaps to be cutting edge research but psychology is not even at a level to understand the education hinders the mind and thus effects the perception and thus the psychology of a being so psychology is in fact not even at a level of being able to make obvious cause and effect connections relative to education. Another way to look at it is psychology is the study of the mind by beings that have no business being in psychology until they at least can understand the core issues relative to psychology which is the perception altering education the beings they "study" get when they are children and the perception altering education said psychologist got when they were children. That a nice way of saying the only beings the psychologists have any business prescribing pills to are their self. If one cannot see fire or detect fire it is possible they are on fire. If one cannot detect how deep the water is it is probable they never left the surface. When you apply the remedy you have done your job and until then you are just a candidate for the job. When I detect a ghost, a lizard man, or an alien I will discuss those topics but until then I only discuss perception. The less details the better. A grounded way to look at this situation is humans were very intelligent but that intelligence allowed them to write a check(invention) their minds couldn't cash. Human beings invented written education and math and are five thousand years into propagating that invention and are just now understanding the mind.

propagating : promote widely.

Another way to look at it is human beings invented something five thousand years before we were ready for it and that is what makes the situation so complicated. Human beings could not understand the mind without math and written education perhaps but the written education and math hindered the mind so human beings can not understand the mind. The situation is a perfect nightmare because the remedy is fear not and the education makes one very afraid or timid. It is like telling a person who cannot swim to swim. It is like telling a person afraid of heights to climb a mountain. It is like telling a person who hates liver to eat liver. It is like telling a person who is afraid of shadows to seek shadows. The one thing a scribe has to do is the one thing that is least probable they will do. The equation remains the same:

X = Scribes
Y = scribes that apply the remedy
Z = children who get the education and become scribes
A = majority
B = remedy
X > Y
X = A

A = Z
A > B

All this is saying is the remedy is very harsh and so
the amount of people that get the education and need
to apply the remedy is always greater than the people
who apply the remedy and in turn the majority always
votes to make sure the children get the education and
they never suggests the remedy because they are not
aware of it. The scribes do not think putting your
hand on a hot stove will burn you. When too much
change is required to solve a problem the problem is
fatal. If the water pouring into the boat is less than the
water being bailed out of the boat the boat will sink. If
modern society came out and said "Written education
and math has detrimental mental consequences" there
would be absolute anarchy and a control structure
seeks the illusion of safety. It is along the logic lines
of "We can't tell the common people that because
there will be an uproar." What this suggests is truth
or morals are secondary to safety and control and that
is stupidity and a symptom of fear. There was a time
in our history where there was chaos and an everyone
for their self mentality and anything goes and that is
similar to how the tribes in the Amazon live now and
they survive. One is either free or a slave and that is
the problem with civilization. As one becomes more
"civilized" one becomes less free yet freedom itself is
civilized so civilized means in some respects tyranny.
Just like the physicist said "If we considered the reality
of what probability suggests we would probably not
get much done." We are not getting much done but
we are creating one hell of an illusion of getting much
done. I listened to the three oil executives in part on
television and they were before congress and they were

all blaming each other and they were doing that for only one reason: money. It is as if a person could go set fire to a forest and burn it down and go to jail but these companies could go burn down a forest and pay their way out of it. A person can't buy justice but a company can, but a company is people. I don't look at the oil slick as anything but a symptom and the reaction from people is also a symptom. People are concerned about cleaning up the oil slick so it will not look so bad so they can retain the possibility they will be able to drill again soon. I detect schizophrenia. I detect society is eager to drill for oil and then eager to clean up the spill and then eager to drill for oil and then eager to clean up the spill. Someone in society has determined oil is more important than life itself so I ponder why they would clean up the oil slick. The oil is clearly more important than the eco system and everyone knows that because if it was not we would not ever risk an oil slick by drilling or transporting oil in the ocean or perhaps only a lunatic would do that. As the saying in the east goes "If you want to be evil be infinitely evil." That's a nice way of saying don't be a half ass or lukewarm. Why are we killing off the environment and thus ourselves slowly? Are we timid? The same people who suggest save the environment are the same people who have no clue to the implications of education on the minds of children so obviously they do not know their head from the hole their head is in. If you want to go through life under the assumption money is of value then do anything you have to do to get all the money. If money is your salvation do whatever you have to do to get it and get all of it and never settle. Beg borrow and steal into infinity if money is your salvation. Drill an oil well every hundred meters in the ocean and you will have lots of money. Do not even put safety values on the oil caps because it costs too much money and do not clean up the oil slicks because that costs too much money. It costs too much money to be concerned about the environment and also be concerned about making money. Maybe we make improper decisions and appear quite odd in our decision making processes because of this:

"What it comes down to is that modern society discriminates against the right hemisphere." - Roger Sperry (1973) Neurobiologist, Nobel Winner

It is not good or bad that you are totally insane and your sense of time proves that, it just is. It is not good or bad that a pill will never cure you of your induced insanity, it is just is. It is not good or bad that society turned you from a sound minded being into an exceptionally insane being with their "wisdom" education, it just is. It is not good or bad that you have to mindfully kill yourself to get your infinitely wise mind back, it just is. It is not good or bad your reasoning ability is everything in the universe but reasonable, it just is. It is not good or bad I have an infinite advantage over you, it just is. It is not good or bad I am bending spoons, it just is. Listening is relative to control as thinking is relative to freedom. You would be wise to stop reading this diary now.
There are no stupid questions just people who cannot understand the answers.

May 13, 2010 (6:09pm) - There is a concept called the trinity. The trinity aspects are the father, the son and the holy ghost and the holy ghost is considered very important. Roger Sperry attempted to explain this holy ghost when he said "When the brain is whole, the unified consciousness of the left and right hemispheres adds up to more than the individual properties of the separate hemispheres."

The equation would look like this.
X = left hemisphere traits = 50 = Son
Y = right hemisphere traits = 50 = Father = most powerful of the two hemispheres relative to traits.
Z = the combined power when hemispheres are unified = 200 = holy ghost
X + Y = Z

The complexity is if one favors the left hemisphere with the education then the equation will not work and the holy spirit aspect will not be achieved. The remedy allows the holy spirit aspect to be achieved again. Another way to look at it is the written education and math eliminates the possibility of the holy spirit aspect unless the remedy is applied after the education. So logically 50 + 50 = 200 appears odd but it is happening and it is real. The sum of left and right hemisphere when in harmony relative to lateralization creates an aspect that is greater than the sum parts of left and right hemisphere.
This is why this comment is so true:
[Mark 3:29 But he that shall blaspheme against the Holy Ghost hath never forgiveness, but is in danger of eternal damnation:]

If one messes up this Holy Ghost aspect of consciousness they are doomed and education does that very efficiently and the remedy restores the Holy Ghost aspect very efficiently. Human beings cannot survive on the sum parts of left hemisphere and they cannot survive on the sum parts of right hemisphere. Human beings are only viable with the Holy Ghost aspect which is beyond the sums of left and right hemisphere and can only be accomplished when left and right hemisphere are at equal strength. That is not a probability that is an absolute. There is only one way to get that holy spirit aspect back after one gets the education and you perhaps do not want to hear it. Let's just say it is best for human beings to have both hemispheres working at full power like they are when one is born. A human being can cut their self and it is probable that cut will heal and they will not be worse for wear because of that cut but the education is messing up the mental harmony and no matter what, that is going to be a nightmare and one may never recover from that. It is not probable the mind can heal itself after twelve years of left brain favoring education and that is evident because very few human beings in the five thousand years since written education was invented have been able to fully restore their mind after the education. There are some that partially restore it but I do not detect there are many that fully restore the mind. I am pleased with the story of Jesus where he touched a tree and the tree died because this story is suggesting on that particular day Jesus did not tell that person/tree the remedy or he did not feel like explaining the remedy properly and that person /tree was doomed.

Giving everyone the benefit of the doubt means ones explains the full measure remedy exactly how it is with no sugar coating because the seekers and the meek will pick it up and run and there is nothing that can stop them and they are the only probable candidates for the remedy, they are showing symptoms of "waking up". That is as good as it gets because we are not talking about a belief system here. We are talking about the probability a human being that has had their mind go through major left brain conditioning trauma starting at the age of six and continuing for many years can restore their right brain traits. The whole story about the parable of sower is if you tell the remedy to five thousand people maybe twelve will understand it and apply it fully. It is not probable the billions of people who suggest they are religious have mindfully killed their self and in fact it is probable they have no idea that is what the religions are saying; a remedy to the tree of knowledge, education. I am not so fantastic because I applied the remedy by accident so relative to my perception I have to say if I can do it anyone can do it but I am in a bubble. In reality it is not easy to apply the remedy but as long as you understand the concepts of the remedy you can experiment with it and if you accidentally apply the remedy it is a miracle. It is not important how many people say it is not a miracle if you apply the remedy, I say it is a miracle and so it is a miracle. Another miracle is the wise beings in the ancient texts wrote down the remedy in one fashion or another and it survived. Fear not, that's a miracle. Walk through the valley of the shadow of death and fear not, that's a miracle. Those who lose their life mindfully preserve it, that's a miracle. Submit, that's a miracle. Go sit in a cemetery alone at night and meditate, that's a miracle. Those are miracles because those concepts are the only ways to fully restore one's mind after getting the education. If a being can actually apply one of those miracles it is another miracle unto itself. I don't need to hear about hocus pocus miracles, these are real miracles. When you are walking around asking yourself "How big was that Mac truck that hit me?" after you apply the remedy, you will understand what a miracle is and you will understand what the Holy Ghost is and perhaps not until.

Miracle: a remarkable and very welcome occurrence.

It is quite remarkable a being can undo all that left brain favoring conditioning with a one second mental self control thought relative to denying ones perception during "action".

9:02 AM 5/14/10 - So the Holy Spirit aspect is achieved when left and right hemisphere are at equal strength and when this happens the sum of the two hemispheres is greater than that parts of the two hemispheres and this state of mind is known in the ancient texts as being filled with the spirit and is also what heaven is. This means hell is anything other than that holy spirit state of mind. The holy spirit state of mind is simply the perfect state of mind and perfect is relative to not lacking anything essential and that is simply sound mind. So hell is the place of suffering because hell is lacking something essential. So the education favors left hemisphere and in turn veils right hemisphere and in turn throws one out of heaven into hell and one is suffering because the holy spirit aspect is negated or not possible until the remedy is applied. I do not detect the scribes that make trillions of dollars off the ancient texts are going to agree with that. One way to look at this situation is to say the education has mentally hindered you and there is a way to undo that mental hindering. Another way to look at it is because you have been mentally hindered by the education you are a threat to yourself and those around you. By threat I mean you get to make decisions. A person that is mentally hindered can make improper decisions or decisions that are unsound. One unsound decision is a mentally hindered person may decide to mentally hinder a child with the education like they were hindered and not even be aware the education hinders the mind and then also not even be aware of the remedy to the mental hindering the education causes and then we have statistics like this as a result:

"Suicide is the 11th leading cause of death in the United States." - CDC: National Suicide Statistics at a Glance

This statistic is the result of beings that are mentally hindered being allowed to make decisions. A being that is mentally hindered relative to cognitive ability will vote to kill other people and they will not even believe that is what they vote for.

"Among the deceased who had mental health problems, 74.9 percent had received a diagnosis of depression/dysthymia, 14.5 percent had been bipolar disorder and

114

8.1 percent had an anxiety disorder, according to the report."

I will explain to you why this is not a suicide statistic this is a homicide statistic. The education favors left hemisphere and veils right hemisphere traits. One of those right hemisphere traits is random access thought patterns. When those random access thought patterns are working properly in the conscious state of mind a mental state of depression is not possible at all. Other words a person in sound mind has these random access thoughts changing so swiftly an actual mental state of depression is not possible. Another way to look at it is the mind cannot maintain any set mental pattern for more than a moment so one can look at it like one is mentally always in neutral on a scale of an hour relative to a clock. This means a state of depression where a person becomes mindful of killing their self because of being depressed literally is not possible. That means this [74.9 percent had received a diagnosis of depression] can only be caused by the fact these beings got the education, have right brain random access traits veiled , were able to achieve prolonged mental thoughts of depression and that turned into a mental thought of suicide and that is why they killed their self. So these people killed their self because they were mentally hindered by the education as a children by law and that means they are homicides.

These other aspects [14.5 percent had been bipolar disorder and 8.1 percent had an anxiety disorder] are relative to the mental hindering also. It is probable some of these people may have been suffering from a terminal illness and took their own life but that would be the only exception or the only situation where one could say that their death was not really from depression, they perhaps just did not want to suffer physically any longer. If you take a child and condition them mentally and later they run into mental problems and then kill their self that is not suicide that is homicide. Another way to look at it is, a person gets the education and because it takes them out of this heaven state of mind they are in turn put in the hell state of mind and so they suffer and at times the suffering is too great and the person determines it is best to kill their self and that is also homicide. If I drip water on your forehead until you can no longer take it and you kill yourself that is homicide. If I give you a drug that alters your perception and you end up killing yourself as a result of your perception being altered that is homicide. I was depressed for ten years and in deep depression and then I accidentally applied the remedy and I have not had one minute, relative to a clock, of depression since so I am fully aware that depression was caused by the fact my random access right brain traits were veiled and after applying the remedy they were restored and now I cannot achieve anything close to a state of depression and I am mindful you may not be able to grasp that truth. I will put it this way, all of your experts do not even know what the tree of knowledge is so clearly you have no experts you simply have the blind leading the blind further into blindness. Although your cult leader will say you are going to hell if you do not do as we say and give us money so we can continue to tell people they are going to hell if they do not "Give us money and do as we say.", I suggest you are not going to hell you are in hell, the place of suffering, you are not at full mental capacity so you are factually suffering. A form of suffering in the place of suffering is not being able to tell one is suffering. It is a very simple equation, perhaps.

Y = extreme left brain state of mind
Z = age when the mind is fully developed
A = education technology

A + Z = Y

The reason a person in the place of suffering cannot tell they are suffering is because they were placed in the place of suffering long before their mind even developed so their mental development was aborted. Looking at the mind as a straight line and this line is slowly bent to the left over several years during the education and in turn the cognitive and mental development never happens. Another way to look at it is that straight line has to keep going straight until the age of 25 when cognitive ability is matured relative to the frontal lobe but the education pushes that straight line off course and it never reaches development point and then when the remedy is applied the mind is already matured so one just restores their mind and then one learns so much so fast they perceive they are in a progression but in reality they just restored their right hemisphere traits so they can "see". I once was blind but now I see simply means I got the education, tree of knowledge, and some senses in my mind, intuition, complexity, ambiguity, were turned off or veiled and then I applied the remedy and restored them and now I have all my senses back and I can "see". I once was lost but now am found , I once was blind but now I see and all that means is one applies the remedy and restores their right hemisphere traits to full power and this enables the holy spirit or third mind aspect. Since we are just a species that invented something with our vast intelligence that just so happens to have mentally hindered us drastically to the point we are factually killing ourselves because we are mentally hindered that is not really that rare. We have invented lots of things that have killed us or harmed us like machine guns for example. I do not detect there are many other species on this planet that are feeling the wrath of the machine gun but we sure are. One way to look at it is since we invented written language and math and in learning those inventions it mentally hindered our cognitive ability we tend to invent things from time to time that only serve to harm us more. If you give a drunk guy a machine gun with a hair trigger he probably will harm himself or harm others and that is essentially as a spices what we are and what we do. A person may suggest they do not harm children or do not harm their own children but the very fact they are not aware the education does mentally destroy a child and the fact they are not aware of that means they are also not aware of the remedy to negate that mental harm means they know not what they do. One does not have to believe they are harming children with the education because they factually are. If you do not believe reading writing and math favors the left hemisphere it does not matter because it still does. If you do not believe the frontal lobe relative to cognitive ability does not develop until one is well over twenty it does not matter because it still does. If you do not believe the remedy works it does not matter because it still does. I only applied the remedy once and it worked flawlessly. The remedy worked so well I should be illegal based on principle alone. I have no sense of time so I cannot relate to how long five thousand years is but I am aware I have systematically reached the core fundamental problem of the species that goes back five thousand years and I have also understood the remedy to the core fundamental problem of the spices that goes back five thousand years and I do not detect any other being on this planet that has done that to the degree they would write books explaining it in detail and that is a testament to how powerful this third mind or holy spirit aspect is and has nothing to do with my genes. It will never be about my genes, it is simply this right hemisphere aspect, the god image in man, is far more powerful than we give it credit for. We invented something that inadvertently turned off the most valuable hemisphere in our mind. For example if you only had right hemisphere working and left hemisphere was veiled to a subconscious state you would not be able to achieve depression or anxiety because your thoughts would be lightning fast and random access so those states of prolonged anxiety or depression would simply not be possible. That's a nice way of saying we could not have messed up our minds worse with our wisdom inventions. We invented something that hindered the one aspect of our mind that is the most valuable and so we could not have harmed ourselves any worse. Supernatural is not going to make reading, writing and math not favor the left hemisphere. Supernatural is not going to make the frontal lobe relative to cognitive ability not mature until well after the age of twenty. I have no issues with saying seeking the shadow of death and then when it arrives fear not, is really mental suicide or mentally killing yourself or mentally detaching or mentally letting go of everything because it does not matter how I put it at all. We as a species are a little bit past the point of sugar coating things relative to the education technology situation.

Time has an "I" and "me" in it.

[1 Thessalonians 5:7 For they that sleep sleep in the night; and they that be drunken are drunken in the night.]

They that sleep in the night are the scribes (sleep means mentally hindered), and thus drunken in the night means they are pleased in that mentally hindered perception dimension. One is blind until they apply the remedy to the education because right brain intuition is a sense or eyes and that is veiled by the education and thus one may see the light as darkness because they are blind or "drunk". The scribes could never figure out what the tree of knowledge is because the darkness sees the light as darkness and the texts are light. There are two people sleeping in bed and the sun comes up and one sees the sun and wakes up and one sees the sun as the darkness and stays asleep because he is drunk in the night or pleased with the night.

[Galatians 6:3: For if a man think himself to be something, when he is nothing, he deceiveth himself.]

For if a man think himself to be something, when he is nothing, he deceiveth himself. = Pride = ego = a side effect of the tree of knowledge, which means right hemisphere is not a good judge so one sees their self as nothing but the education veils that so one sees their self as something.

The scribes saw Jesus as a liar and a fool and anyone who got the education and has not applied the remedy is a scribe factually : [Matthew 9:3 And, behold, certain of the scribes said within themselves, This man blasphemeth.]

That is logical because after the education one is in the place of suffering the alternate perception dimension and they would see light as darkness, truth as lies and reason as insanity.

5/15/10 12:17 AM - This section is concepts and simply homework or calculations so it is not set in stone but it is a pondering. Firstly when one applies the remedy they have no sense of time so they are in infinity and that is how a person starts off in life in the sound mind state. Then the education pushes one into the sense of time state of perception so life seems very short. So the scribes think life is very short and in the no sense of time dimension life seems infinitely long. Another way to look at it is one cannot tell how long life is no matter what, it is not possible. So physics suggest time is relative which means it is not fixed and depends on the observer. So one can look at it like every human is what was called an angel. In this location every angel tends to get the education and then they become dark angels but sometimes an angel applies the remedy and they go back to being a light angel. Sometimes one of the light angels applies the remedy so well they become an Arch angel and sometimes a dark angel becomes a leader and they become an Arch angel. All angels die but the harmony in this scenario is the light angels always lose and the dark angels always win because it is the nature of the light angels to be meek and carefree and not ashamed and not afraid and so humans are perhaps angels and if they never got the education they would be just carefree. The complexity is the humans still in nature are pure angels and they show symptoms of that because they just live off the land and do not make a fuss and they are not perfect but they also are not militant in contrast to the dark angels, the scribes.

This line suggests an angel has no pride or ego so they would not be ashamed of anything.
They are nothing. They do not see their self as great or of great value and that is relative to no ego.
[Genesis 2:25 And they were both naked, the man and his wife, and were not ashamed.]
[Galatians 6:3 For if a man think himself to be something, when he is nothing, he deceiveth himself.]

This second line is saying if a person which may be an angel thinks they are something they are wrong they are nothing and this is shown in the Genesis comment. A light angel is just a servant so they would not be ashamed of things like nudity because that would mean they think they are something. Think about natives that still live in the wild and a scribe goes up to them and sees them naked and thinks "They should be ashamed" but the natives are not ashamed because they do not see their self as having value or they see their self as nothing relative to ego. This nothingness aspect is why the native tribes were taken advantage of, they did not really fight back against the dark angels, the scribes. So once in a while a dark angel which is one that got the education falls from grace relative to the dark side or they quit the dark side and they have to be in "society" so then they become an arch angel on the light side and they fight against the dark angels in "society". Other word's there has perhaps never been a case where a tribe has attacked society in any meaningful way relative to waging an all out war on all of society, the society of the scribes the dark angels. For example the Native Americans did not try to conquer Europe and the Native Africans did not try to conquer Europe or enslave Europeans. So this explains why the dark angels always win and get to turn all the children from light angels into dark angels simply because the light angels are carefree and do not even take their self seriously at all because they have no shame or pride or ego.

[Genesis 19:1 And there came two angels to Sodom at even; and Lot sat in the gate of Sodom: and Lot seeing them rose up to meet them; and he bowed himself with his face toward the ground;]

These may be an arch angels which are scribes that applied the remedy well and Lot is just an angel a light angel but not an arch angel. So this place we call planet earth is perhaps the battle ground and although we can call it many things the bottom line is all atoms are made up of 99.9% empty space. So we are 99.9% empty space and that is very close to nothing.

[Galatians 6:3 For if a man(scribe) think himself to be something(has pride and ego), when he is nothing(had no pride and ego before the tree of knowledge education), he deceiveth himself(and should apply the remedy so he is not hallucinating so much).]

So this whole concept of armies of angels fighting and each army being led by an arch angel means the scribes versus the tribes but they are not scribes versus the tribes they are the dark angels versus the light angels and light angels usually lose because they are just angels without ego or pride so a victory means nothing. If one really wants to win that is a symptom of ego and pride and that is why the dark angels usually win in the long run because they have pride and ego and so they lust to win. Another way to look at it is, if one has no sense of time they are factually in infinity and it is not important if a person that senses time believes that because time is relative. Anyone who applies the remedy the full measure will lose their sense of time and it is understood fact that people with right brain heavy traits so to speak cannot sense time so they are in the infinity state of perception. So we were all light angels living in this place and then written education and math came about maybe created by humans/angels that wanted to be better which is a symptom of ego and pride and everything went bad. An angel with no ego and no pride does not seek to be better they are kind of just well, nothing. Go with the flow, absent minded, funny, hard to pin down, hard to understand, strange behavior. Other words a light angel is not God it is just a funny little creature that is care free and has no concept of shame or guilt or self and so contrary to that aspect is, a dark angel has pride, ego, greed, lust, envy, wrath and all of those traits are why the dark angels win out over the light angels. In order for the light angels to win they have to have lust or greed to win and they have to have wrath to win and they are not capable of that. The saying goes "It is easy as taking candy from a baby." and that means a baby is not greedy or lustful for that candy and so someone who is greedy can easily trick that baby and take their candy but that's only because that baby is care free or without ego. So this means we may not be humans we just call ourselves humans, we are perhaps the angels in infinity and some angels eat this tree of knowledge and become dark angels that sense time and so everything seems fast as in life goes fast but life doesn't go fast it is just relative to their perception because they ate off the tree of knowledge and it made them perceive things in infinity that gives them the impression this not infinity but once they apply the remedy they see it is infinity again. Once in a while a dark angel wakes up by applying the remedy and is among the dark angels but is a light angel and they appear special or odd but only in contrast to the dark angels. These are known as Saints, Prophets and other things and one pattern is many are often killed for one reason or another but they do not always resist or they go willingly and that is because they have no ego or pride. So an atom is mostly empty space but it takes up space so most space is empty space. A hole in this concept is normal mammals don't sense time either and perhaps all animals don't sense time at least ones with brains. If other animals sensed time then they would build for the future but even in cases like squirrels, they save nuts for the winter but they often lose track of where they put them and that is in line with this absent minded professor state of memory one has when right brain is unveiled. One way to look at it is in the machine state there is no five minutes ago so what happen five minutes ago does not register in the mind. The machine state is a machine state and contrary a scribe that has a very pronounced sense of time and that is a left brain trait so they should be able to remember well what happened a year ago or five minutes ago. The whole premise of recorded history is man started recording historical events which denotes sense of time and that happened after the invention of written language but is not a symptom of written language it is a symptom written language made man start sensing time because in learning written language one has to favor left hemisphere and that hemisphere is great at sensing time, judgment. This is deep but maybe

126

the universe is a fish bowl and we are fish in that bowl and when we are at full strength mentally we do not detect we are of value at all and so maybe we are just like a side project and then we messed around with language and it made us weird but we are still nothing but fish in a fish bowl but our extreme ego and pride aspects make us think we are something. It does not make sense the tribes that never got written education and math that are around today are living in nature and off of nature and they are abnormal or their behavior is abnormal because we do not even know how long they have really been living like that but we do know for example the aborigines lived like that for 60,000 years relative to a calendar and they did not destroy the planet in that time but the scribes have pretty much destroyed the ecological system in under 5000 years. There are two totally different perceptions happening in those two types of humans, one is very aggressive compared to the other. The ones that still live in nature are very docile in contrast to the scribes and it is perhaps very hard to suggest they are not very docile in contrast to scribes. As a species we are so far down this sense of time perception road the way back is daunting. The only feasible solution is to not change anything but our perception which means apply the remedy. If we can just get to a point where we suggest the education may have some unwanted mental side effects that alone is a total victory because it opens up a door that we can look into, but of course if one applies the remedy they will see very clearly anyway. so to speak. There is not much purpose in getting too far ahead since we still as a species do not think the education does anything unwanted to the mind. As a species our stance on reading, writing and math is, there cannot be anything wrong with them at all, so we are not in a position to do much until we at least get to the point of questioning that assumption.

5/15/10 1:53 PM - If you flip this remedy aspect around one can perhaps see the test aspect of it. Something is challenging you. Something is saying I bet you do not have what it takes to seek the shadow of death and when it arrives you do not fear it and in fact you are indifferent to it. Something is saying I bet you cannot lose your life mindfully or let go of life when you perceive your life is in peril. I bet you cannot submit to the full measure, so from that point of view one can see this remedy is a gauntlet that is on everyone's plate that gets the education and some look at it as a challenge and some will not get near that challenge. Something is telling you to your face on a universal scale you can't apply this remedy. You do not have what it takes to apply this remedy and you will not ever be able to accomplish this remedy. From that point of view something is not saying you have to do this remedy it is saying you are not capable of doing this remedy and that changes the entire mechanics of the remedy because children do not like to be told what they cannot do. It is not even important what it is but a child refuses to be told what to do and will resist. So instead of looking at it like you have to apply the remedy one can look at it like they have to resist not applying the remedy. There is a cookie, the remedy, in a jar and appears to be out of reach and someone says "Do not eat that cookie." No one can stop you from grabbing that cookie but you because as a human being you can do whatever you want to do no matter what. There is nothing in the universe that can stop you from grabbing that cookie or grabbing that gauntlet but you. It is possible for any being to pull the sword from the stone it is just not probable every being will pull the sword from the stone. Be mindful in the story of Job one aspect was speaking to another aspect and said "I do not think Job has what it takes." and the other aspect replied in spirit "Is that so?" Control tends to be administered under the guise of safety. Sometimes pinprick minds make fun of minds they cannot prick.

[Matthew 7:29 For he taught them as one having authority, and not as the scribes.] - The spirit of this comment is saying Jesus was a good guy unlike those scribes. It is a jab at the scribes. Jesus was everything in the universe but like the scribes, so to speak. The problem with that is there were many scribes. This is another jab at the scribes much earlier in the texts:

[Jeremiah 8:8 How do ye say, We are wise, and the law of the LORD is with us? Lo, certainly in vain made he it; the pen of the scribes is in vain.]

So if one combines the two comments in a way they are saying Jesus was not like the scribes because the scribes are vain and the Lord, right hemisphere, is not with them.

Do not give your child this education on the premise of money or popularity or for the promise of luxury and then not assist them with the remedy or our species will become an abomination.= [Leviticus 19:29 Do not prostitute thy daughter, to cause her to be a whore; lest the land fall to whoredom, and the land become full of wickedness.]

Neitche said "A casual stroll around the lunatic asylum shows faith proves nothing." I get a kick out of that one, lunatic asylum means the place the scribes built, the tower to heaven. It is perhaps not possible to stop the curse and it is perhaps not possible to stop trying to stop the curse. That suggests it may just be a test with no solution.

[Genesis 3:4 And the serpent(Imhotep) said unto the woman, Ye shall not surely die:(if you get the education or written language and you can trust me because my name Imhotep means "one who comes in peace" and my god is a four headed ram god.)

5/16/10 12:07 PM -

"Imhotep was associated with Thoth, the Egyptian god of writing, education, literacy and scribes through the Greco-Roman Period which refers to those geographical regions and countries who culturally (and so historically) were directly, protractedly and intimately influenced by the language, culture, government and religion of the ancient Greeks and Romans." - Wikipedia.Com

Culture is relative to writing, education, literacy and scribes. So relative to the time period there were tribes and scribes and they were adversaries. As time went on the tribes discovered they could not compete with the scribes so the tribes came up with methods to negate the mental hindering caused by learning the script and this was known as the covenant or "repent". So one was born into the culture of the scribes and they were taught writing, math and literacy and then one would repent which means they applied the remedy and then one attempted to convince other scribes to "repent". The complexity is after one gets the writing and math they were mentally hindered, insane, lacking cognitive ability and so the remedy was not about "do as I say" it was just reasonable to not want to be insane when one did not have to be. Of course convincing an insane person they are insane is essentially impossible or improbable. For example the tribes attempted to suggest to the Ruler scribes there were problems associated with learning the education and even to this day no one has been able to convince the ruler scribes in civilization of this and that is an indication an insane person probably cannot reason or cannot make obvious connections relative to cause and effect relationships. It is similar to telling a person that fire will burn them but that person is no longer able to make that connection so they will perhaps burn their self and burn others around them and never be able to mentally grasp that is what is happening. Modern society is asking this question : "Why are there such bad emotional problems and drug problems and people harming each other and environmental problems?" and modern society cannot grasp it is because that education has made everyone insane because they do not apply the remedy after the education and so the scribes are not able to viably exist with their self, their surroundings or those around them.

Does the species want to have all these emotional problems? No. Then why do they continue to create them using the education to hinder the mind and that creates the emotional problems? Because the Rulers of modern society got the education and they are insane and have no cognitive ability to even figure out the education is what causes the emotional problems if the remedy is not applied after one gets the education. Simply put after the education if one does not apply the remedy they are factually insane and if they are allowed to make decisions they will make insane decisions unless they make a decision they think is foolish and that foolish decision will tend to be a wise decision. For example to a scribe it would seem very foolish to stop educating children until any potential problems caused by education can be understood and so they would never vote to do that, but if they did they would perceive that was foolish but in absolute reality that would be very wise. Once a problem is identified it is wise to stop creating more problems by continuing that problem creating aspect; stop everything and understand the scope of the problem but this problem is caused by to literacy, writing and math so that decision appears foolish and stupid to the scribes because they see wisdom as foolishness. I hear one comment more than any from the scribes in my experiments and it is "What do you think we should stop educating children?" and what they are really saying is "What do you think we should stop mentally hindering children?" but they factually have no idea that is really what they are saying at all. The scribes are asking me if I think we should stop mentally ruining children as if that is a question that needs to be asked and what is more troubling relatively speaking is when I say "Yes" they say "You are crazy." The scribes just have determined educated means "good" when in reality "educate " mean's harm. The scribes are asking "You think we should stop educating (harming) children?" as if that is some profound earth shattering brain teaser. The scribes cognitive ability is so destroyed they actually ask me if I think we should stop mentally ruining the children. If reading writing and math is more important than the mental well being of children then we are a species that has simply lost all cognitive ability and thus whatever happens is just as well relative to our species. We have progressed into the mental curse to the stage now we mentally kill all the children and as a collective species we do not even believe that or are no longer even able to question if that is what we are doing so we are far past any stage of recovery so we are in the stage of extinction. Even after typing that certain scribes will say "That is not true'" and then tomorrow they will sit on their hands and vote to make sure all the children continue to get the "education" and never even consider suggesting to the children the potential mental effects of the education nor suggesting the remedy. The scribes would at least show symptoms of mercy if they told the children up front all that left brain favoring education may have some mental side effects considering the child's cognitive ability relative to the frontal lobe does not mature until well after the age of twenty but they do not show any symptoms of mercy or compassion at all. The scribes, the ones that sense time are either so diabolical or under the influence of something so sinister they cannot even "see" the darkness at all or they have been conditioned into a state of insanity that keeping them isolated from everyone else is the only logical solution. One does not have the luxury of mercy when faced with rabidity or when in the grips of rabidity.

[Genesis 4:13 And Cain said unto the LORD, My punishment is greater than I can bear.

Genesis 4:14 Behold, thou hast driven me out this day from the face of the earth; and from thy face shall I be hid; and I shall be a fugitive and a vagabond in the earth; and it shall come to pass, that every one that findeth me shall slay me.

Genesis 4:15 And the LORD said unto him, Therefore whosoever slayeth Cain, vengeance shall be taken on him sevenfold. And the LORD set a mark upon Cain, lest any finding him should kill him.

Genesis 4:16 And Cain went out from the presence of the LORD, and dwelt in the land of Nod, on the east of Eden.

Genesis 4:17 And Cain knew his wife; and she conceived, and bare Enoch: and he builded a city, and called the name of the city, after the name of his son, Enoch.] =

Consequences for eating off of the tree of knowledge and not applying the remedy and also the consequences of making the children eat off the tree of knowledge and never suggesting the remedy to them. The concept in this short passage is in fact what modern society is.

[a fugitive and a vagabond in the earth] = out of harmony with their environment = rabidity = insane = no longer viable because one is no longer mentally viable. Cain is the scribes.

[thou hast driven me out this day from the face of the earth] = One is no longer able to coexist with their environment or one is in conflict with their self, their own species, their environment and in turn it is probable ones longevity is everything in the universe but certain. The mental harmed caused by the education is just like a computer virus.

X = the virus
Y = computers on the network
Z = anti-virus software

X + Y = Modern society
X + Z = ones that applied the remedy

The concept of contact simply means a child is in perfect mental harmony or in the now when they are born and so that means they are very easily influenced. If that child associates with an adult that has the virus they will get the virus and then if that child applies the remedy they will be immune to the virus. The problem is the remedy may take a person the rest of their life to apply if they are timid and this is what this line suggests.

[and from thy face shall I be hid] In sequence [I shall be hid from they face.]

This line of course is out of sequence which is a signpost the being that wrote this line has right brain aspects unveiled or at least the being that suggested this line did.

[Hid] denotes fear or timidity and it also suggests God no longer acknowledges the scribes, Cain. Along the lines of "see no evil". This is just suggesting the scribes got the education and did not apply the remedy so their right hemisphere aspects are veiled and so they mentally cannot achieve the third mind mental aspect called the Holy Spirit , which is when the mind is in harmony it creates a third mental aspect that combines the two hemisphere aspects to make up a third aspect greater than the sum of the sum of the two hemisphere aspects, and since the scribes are not capable of achieving that until they apply the remedy, they are cut off from God.

[that every one that findeth me shall slay me.] This line in part suggest the scribes are outcasts and it is not so much the ones that apply the remedy do not like them because after all the scribes were born in perfect harmony but were turned "bad" by the adult scribes, it is more like they are mocked on an unseen level yet the ones who apply the remedy see that mocking easily.

This is mocking scribes : [Matthew 9:3 And, behold, certain of the scribes said within themselves, This man blasphemeth.] It is saying the scribes thought Jesus was bad or evil or foolish and that conclusion requires great mental blindness. One has to have a pretty laughable cognitive ability to conclude Jesus was a fool or a liar and the scribes concluded he was.

This is mocking the scribes: [Jeremiah 8:8 How do ye say, We are wise, and the law of the LORD is with us? Lo, certainly in vain made he it; the pen of the scribes is in vain.]
It is saying "Tell me about your great wisdom scribes now that the god image in man, right hemisphere is veiled and no longer factors into your perception and since perception is relative to cognitive ability, your sense of time proves you have no cognitive ability. So please great wise scribes tell me your vast wisdom you have so I may learn from your vast backwards wisdom."

[How do ye say, We are wise]. One cannot possibly be wise ever into infinity if their right hemisphere traits are veiled to a subconscious state, or even slightly because that slight veiling negates the chance of the third mind aspect, is what the education does and the scribes sense of time proves their right hemisphere traits are veiled to a subconscious state. There is no mercy for the wicked, the scribes, it is just the scribes are too blind to see they get no mercy. These ancient texts are not for the scribes to read, or were not intended for scribes consumption because they are like "propaganda" against the scribes but of course the scribes will deny that perhaps.

[Matthew 7:29 For he taught them as one having authority, and not as the scribes.]

This comment is saying in spirit Jesus was everything in the universe but like the scribes, the ones that sense time, Cain.

[And the LORD set a mark upon Cain, lest any finding him should kill him.] Kill is a strange word. If one is being mocked on a scale of thousands of years and they are not even aware of it they are being "killed" or "owned". If one is publishing texts that mock them they are being "outclassed" and "mocked" and "ridiculed."

[And the LORD set a mark upon Cain] = [Genesis 3:14 And the LORD God said unto the serpent, Because thou hast done this, thou art cursed] = cursed = separated from God, the god image in man.

[Mark] = firstly the Egyptians called characters in written language marks. Secondly mark means traits, like strong sense of time, strong sense of hunger, strong emotional capacity so traits like pride, ego, lust, envy can be achieved and maintained. Mark is the suffering caused by having right hemisphere traits veiled and this means the third mind aspect is negated until the remedy is applied, so one suffers because of the "mark". The mark of the beast is strong sense of time, strong sense of hunger, strong emotional capacity like pride, ego, lust, envy, greed and these aspects are simply not possible when right brain is unveiled after one applies the remedy but it is not the being who applies the remedy is so "good", it just is a trait of having the mind in perfect lateralization relative to the hemisphere traits.

So because a scribe is cursed, part of the curse is they cannot even tell they are being mocked over thousands of years on a world stage so they are "missing all the jokes making fun of them." There is no peace, love and happiness while innocent children are being mentally destroyed and there is not ever going to be peace, love, and happiness as long as that continues so get those words out of your vocabulary because those aspects do not happen in this narrow since the "falling out.". Happiness is achieved when a being has buried their mind in the sand to avoid the light of reality or when a being can comprehend any situation that arises.

I am mindful the scribes need proof as I am mindful the scribes do not know what proof is.

[Esther 3:12 Then were the king's scribes called on the thirteenth day of the first month..]

[king's scribes] = the control structures advisors. A Ruler scribe will have all his little advisor scribes. The blind leading others into blindness. It is not probable a scribe advisor would ever suggest the education hinders the mind because then they would have to suggest they were mentally hindered and in turn they would not be an advisor for very long. I am not controlling by telling beings how to apply the remedy to restore their mind, I just like bending spoons perhaps.

[the thirteenth day of the first month] = [Galatians 4:10 Ye observe days, and months, and times, and years.] = sense of time = a perception aspect that is a side effect of having right brain traits veiled. [observe] = perceive.

So [day] and [month] are symptoms of sense of time and the cause of that in part is [thirteen] which denotes a number system , and math favors left hemisphere. It is probable if one contacts beings that still live in nature, the tribes, and that tribe had no contact with the scribe society, they may not have calendars and that would show they have no sense of time and that would be because a number system is needed for a calendar and in learning a number system one veils their right hemisphere and starts sensing time. So this whole control structure of modern society is built upon flawed inventions. Reading, writing and math are inventions that have a major flaws, they veil the right hemisphere and make one insane and unable to reason and unable to achieve cognition until one applies the remedy. A scribe cannot argue with that they can just say perhaps, "Our scribe advisors never told me that so it cannot be true." The blind leading the blind into blindness. Sometimes when a mind cannot understand another mind they assume that mind is foolish. To say something is absurd in a probability universe is absurd. Quick sticks out in a sea of sloth.

The meek can preserve it. Many scribes see the light as darkness and the way as a wall and avoid it. Evil seldom sees far enough ahead to see its own deeds.

5/17/10 8:15 AM -
Somebody said you're not alive until your dead.
Many mocked and several scratched their head.
Could a double line be achieved with such a knife?
From the shade such a matter is made.
Solid rock, just solid sand.
One will be lonely or blind to loneliness.
Some seek grace and some are just busy.
The past was just tomorrows now.
Terror could not see what silence might achieve.
Baskets would not hold the water that could weave.
The business of obsession behind mental recession.
Could a double line be achieved with such a knife?
Their power is the only weakness they fear to lose.
Concerned about fate when trapped in hardened slate.
Run from shadows in bitter hate.
Solid rocks are just solid sand.
Darker regions never grip the hand.
Mouth in line with the foot, mime aligns with the soot.
Recluse of shame denied his fame.

[Daniel 1:1 In the third year of the reign of Jehoiakim king of Judah came Nebuchadnezzar king of Babylon unto Jerusalem, and besieged it.]

This is just saying a Scribe Ruler Nebuchadnezzar made slaves out of the tribes, the ones with no sense of time. This is similar to how the scribes made slaves out of the Africans in recent history and how the scribes took advantage of the Native Americans. This is also similar to why Moses fought against the Pharaoh who would not release the slaves, the tribes he controlled. So we know Nebuchadnezzar was a scribe because he was known to have done lots of construction and engineering such as building many canals and also the Hanging Gardens of Babylon and both feats required math. So Babylon was the name given to civilization just as Sodom and Ghamorra were the names given to civilization. This is not suggesting cities are bad this is suggesting cities are a symptom of the scribes because they require math to build. Along the lines of where there is smoke there is fire.

[came Nebuchadnezzar king of Babylon unto Jerusalem, and besieged it.] = A scribe King took the tribes hostage or made them his slaves. So this story of Daniel starts off by explaining how the scribes attacked the tribes or the scribes took advantage of the tribes. It is saying "We did not attack the scribes they attacked us." The logic is a being with a sound mind tends to live in harmony with their surroundings so instead of trying to control others they tend to try to adapt to others and the scribes are of unsound mind and they are just the reverse, the scribes cannot adapt well so they attempt to make everyone do it their way and that requires controlling others. Another way to look at it the reason this "curse" has gone on so long is the tribes so to speak tend to adapt to it instead of trying to stop it because a sound minded being does not see bad or good, they just see opportunities to come to understandings. That is kind of the fatal flaw of the ones that have no sense of time, they walk around and say "Everything looks good to me." so they must apply self control to see something is wrong and that does not happen often. Because right brain has lots of ambiguity the ones with no sense of time tend to be philosophical about everything and so the scribes who are lacking this ambiguity tend to see everything as good and evil.

[Genesis 2:17 But of the tree of the knowledge of [good and evil], thou shalt not eat of it: for in the day that thou eatest thereof thou shalt surely die.]

So the scribes and the tribes are trapped by their own perception. The tribes tend not to see problems and the scribes tend to see many problems. The tribes are not really out to fix anything and the scribes tend to want to fix everything. The problem with this "fix things" perception is things might not be broken and so in attempting to fix something not broken the scribes break it. For example Nebuchadnezzar built all of these canals and one might suggest that is a great feat and he fixed the river but maybe a river doesn't need to be fixed, maybe the river is just fine as it is and if one builds canals no matter what how well they do it, it will affect the ecological system that existed before the canal was built. Because of that one has to question perhaps did Nebuchadnezzar build those canals to make life easier or did he build those canals to boost his ego and pride? Does man seek to explore space for some benefit besides the ego and pride boost? Does man seek to control others for the others benefit or just so they can say "I am in control."? These are the two extremes, the scribes perceive everything is broken and needs to be fixed and the tribes tend to perceive nothing is broken so leave it alone. So the scribes perception is control based, control what is, and the tribes perception is freedom or leave it as it is, it is not broken. "Don't build canals or irrigation ditches because the river flows the way it does for a reason." What one does with what they perceive is relative to their perception and the scribes nature is to "fix" or control what is, and the tribes nature is to adapt to what is. Based on that concept alone the tribes always lose because they do not want to control the scribes and in part see there is a reason the scribes mentally hinder people with their education, the tree of knowledge. These ancient texts are valuable on one hand because they are thoughts of honest observers.

[Daniel 1:2 And the Lord gave Jehoiakim king of Judah into his hand, with part of the vessels of the house of God: which he carried into the land of Shinar to the house of his god; and he brought the vessels into the treasure house of his god.]

[And the Lord gave Jehoiakim king of Judah into his hand, with part of the vessels of the house of God:]:This is just suggesting the Ark of the covenant which are beings who applied the remedy well were captured by the scribes. [Vessels] denotes containers and beings that apply the remedy well are containers of the word of God which is simply the remedy to the tree of knowledge and/or they have the third mind aspect

144

working. One can look at it like the tribes were invaded and their most valuable treasure the arks, vessels were captured.

So the first line is saying the scribes attacked us, the tribes, and the second line is saying, and the scribes captured the arks, the ones who could explain the remedy or assist others with applying the remedy or ones who applied the remedy well. There is nothing more important than the Arks because as long as one has reading, writing and math they have to have someone who can explain the remedy to those people so this second line says treasure but that is not talking about gold and gems, it is talking about the Arks, the vessels that can explain the remedy or at least applied the remedy and that is far more valuable than gold or gems because these beings had the holy spirit or the third mind aspect working. Daniel is attempting to sound modest and saying "The scribes captured the treasures" and that is logical because they brought the treasures to their treasure house which means their "cities". It would have sounded egotistical if Daniel would have said "and the scribes captured our most valuable treasure, me and my three friends, the arks."

[Daniel 1:3 And the king spake unto Ashpenaz the master of his eunuchs, that he should bring certain of the children of Israel, and of the king's seed, and of the princes;

Daniel 1:4 Children in whom was no blemish, but well favoured, and skilful in all wisdom, and cunning in knowledge, and understanding science, and such as had ability in them to stand in the king's palace, and whom they might teach the learning and the tongue of the Chaldeans.]

This is just a repeat of the second verse with details added.
[Children in whom was no blemish, but well favoured, and skilful in all wisdom] These are beings that got the tree of knowledge and then applied the remedy, so they are skillful in all wisdom because they have a sound mind. Think about society and you see a scribe and they are very good at one thing but are not very good at all things and the reverse is a person of sound mind is a master of adaptation so they can pick up on anything swiftly. This is because right brain does not see labels so a scribe that does see lots of parts might pick a field of study and stay with it and never blend any fields of study. Another way to look at it is if a person's perception sees everything as one thing it is probable they may appear to have many talents but only relative to outside observers. Right brain seeks understandings so a being of sound mind seeks understandings and so everything is on the table because an understanding can be gained from anything or any topic or any field of study and because one is in machine state they are very good at concentration and they learn in real time so they can appear to be [skilful in all wisdom]. Because there is not one single nation on the planet that suggests there is any problems with reading writing and math relative to the mental hindering it is not probable there is any nation on the planet that applies this remedy on its children so this "way of life" has either died off or has gone underground completely. It

is possible the scribes wiped these "tribes"out, tribes meaning human beings that got education and applied the remedy after doing so. The tribes that live in nature and never got education would not know the remedy. So these children of Israel were simply human beings that got the education and then kept the covenant and applied the remedy and their "group" relative to the west was probably wiped out long before the time of Jesus because by the time of Jesus it was all scribes.

[John 2:18 Little children, it is the last time: and as ye have heard that antichrist(scribes) shall come, even now are there many antichrists(scribes); whereby we know that it is the last time.]

[even now are there many antichrists(scribes)]

So in that light one can perhaps see by this comment:
[Luke 1:13 But the angel said unto him, Fear not, Zacharias: for thy prayer is heard; and thy wife Elisabeth shall bear thee a son, and thou shalt call his name John.]

Zacharias was one of the children of Israel and he knew the remedy, fear not, and told his son John the Baptist who was born of a miracle birth by his Mother Elizabeth who was barren or sterile and this started a new revival but this is an indication that the children of Israel(ones in heaven or ones that had the third mind/ Holy Spirit aspect) by that time were essentially all wiped out or the movement had gone underground. The reason it went underground is because anytime these tribes attempted to form a community the scribes would show up and take them over and take advantage of them and the tribes tended not to resist because they are prone to adapt to any situation. Right brain people tend to be taken advantage of because they do not see so much "good and evil", they see everything is for a reason and so these scribes that are extreme left brain and seek control and see good and evil would be prone to take advantage of these tribes. Another way to look at it is lunatics take advantage of sound minded beings because sound minded beings are in mental harmony and thus tend to adapt as in adapt to being taken advantage of by lunatics. It's along the lines of the concept taking candy from a baby. In a true vacuum a person of sound mind is in the machine state, no sense of time and so they have no ego or pride so if someone comes to takes advantage of them it is very easy because resisting being taken advantage of is a symptom of ego and pride. For example Jesus knew he would be killed by the scribes that sent their minion guards to get him and he did not require his disciples protect him and that is proof he had no ego or pride. This is exactly what it is:

[Luke 10:3 Go your ways: behold, I send you forth as lambs(tribes) among wolves(scribes).]

Disharmony (scribes) sees harmony as disharmony and destroys it and harmony sees disharmony and adapts to it. This is the nature of the two mind sets. The scribes are not educating the children because they see the children are smart it is because they see the children as dumb or evil and in need of fixing, for example. It is not the education that is so bad it is just after one gets the education the remedy is very harsh to apply relative to a being that is prone to fear and timid which is what a being is in after they get the education because it makes the hypothalamus very hyper or sensitive. Simply put, go to an abandoned house in the middle of the woods at night alone with no lights and go down into the basement and stay there all night and when the first thought that hits your mind after reading that says "That would be very dangerous" you will understand what a timid nervous wreck the education has made you.

[Daniel 1:5 And the king appointed them a daily provision of the king's meat, and of the wine which he drank: so nourishing them three years, that at the end thereof they might stand before the king.]

This is saying the scribes who captured the arks took very good care of these children of Israel because among other things they were [skilful in all wisdom] and that includes they perhaps knew the remedy and how to explain how people could apply it. The reason these beings were so valuable is because the education mentally alters ones perception and changes ones level of consciousness and level of consciousness is one definition of a dimension, so after one learns the education they are "transported" to an alternate perception dimension and these children of Israel were the only ones that could explain to them how to get back with the fear not remedy so these children of Israel or vessels were more valuable than anything else. If one does not have a way to get back to the normal perception dimension after getting that education they end up with 10% of a mind and so they are dead in the water mentally and so these vessels or arks or children of Israel were of value but to the scribes, Nebuchadnezzar, it was for their "skillful in all wisdom" aspects which is why they were taken care of because they were very valuable "advisors". There is a concept about the chosen, the chosen ones, that is referring to these vessels but on a deeper level, after getting all that left brain education the chances of one getting back to the normal perception dimension fully is slim so it appears they must be chosen by some miracle aspect because it simply does not happen that much. The full measure means one has to lose their life mindfully which means one has to experience perceived death willingly and that is quite a rare thing. It is one thing to have a near death experience but it is another thing to seek a near death experience and then when it arrives submit to it. Other words people apply this remedy to a degree but very few ever apply it fully, this is because one is always a slave to their perception so even ones who apply the remedy partially still cannot tell if they have done it fully and so the only way to fully know one has done it fully is when one loses their sense of time completely. Loss of sense of time completely means right hemisphere traits are back to fifty percent and when that happens this holy spirit aspect is achieved which means the left and right hemisphere traits in perfect harmony create a third aspect that is greater than the sum of the two aspects so it is along the lines of having 100 mass and getting 200 energy out of that mass which defies E=Mc2.

"When the brain is whole, the unified consciousness of the left and right hemispheres adds up to more than the individual properties of the separate hemispheres."
- Roger Sperry

Unified = harmony; in perfect harmony, in perfect lateralization and that can only be achieved after the education by applying the remedy to the full measure. If one has 50 left and 50 right and they add up to 200 then something "spooky" is happening so to speak. Relative to the damaged caused by the education it is a very simple test to determine the damage. If one senses time and one got the education it means the paradox aspect for right hemisphere no longer factors into their conscious perception and until they apply the remedy the full measure and lose sense of time their mind is hindered and they cannot achieve this "third" mind aspect created when the mind is "unified".

[Daniel 1:6 Now among these were of the children of Judah, Daniel, Hananiah, Mishael, and Azariah:]

These names are the Lords or Masters but not necessarily Prophets and in the east they would be known as Buddha. Prophets teach the remedy Lords and Masters just applied the remedy but may not teach the remedy. It is quite risky. The oracle of Delphi said about Socrates "There is none wiser than Socrates." Now that is relative to that hemisphere or influence or that part of the world at the time. These beings [Daniel, Hananiah, Mishael, and Azariah] are so valuable because not only did they get education and math but

151

they also perhaps applied the remedy the full measure so they are a prize for the scribes and a treasure for the tribes. This [and skilful in all wisdom] ,means all knowing, and these arks were all knowing and so they were very valuable. Simply put they could explain to any scribe who got the education how that scribe could apply the remedy if they wished and that scribe would become [skilful in all wisdom]. This is relative to the concept of a spring of infinite wisdom meaning not only were they wise in all areas they were so wise they could make any scribe as wise as they were and so that means they could potentially make every scribe as wise as they were simply by explaining the concepts of the remedy to the scribe and if the scribe follows that direction they would become [skillful in all wisdom]. This skillful in all wisdom aspect has nothing to do with genes; if any person on the planet that got the education or associated with someone who has by "contact" and then they apply this remedy the full measure they will achieve this mental harmony aspect that will create this Holy Spirit third mind mental aspect and they will factually be [skilful in all wisdom] which means there is nothing in the universe they cannot understand and thus master within a short span of moments and that is an indication of how powerful humans minds are when they achieve this "holy spirit" aspect caused by perfect mental harmony. I am not suggesting I am skillful in all wisdom as much as I am suggesting I found out the way you can be skillful in all wisdom. If you perceive that is arrogant then certainly you will be rushing out to apply the remedy just to put me to the test perhaps.

"When the brain is whole, the unified consciousness of the left and right hemispheres adds up to more than the individual properties of the separate hemispheres."
- Roger Sperry

The above comment is not a joke and is not pixie dust it is in fact the occult secret about these huge brains we have; somehow when the hemisphere aspects mentally are in perfect alignment they create a third mind that exceeds the sum parts of the two aspects of the mind and that third mind is so powerful it never stops getting better so it can never be measured. One complexity is a person that never got education and has no contact with the scribes or civilization is already in this third mind aspect state but they do not have written language or math so it is very difficult to communicate with them.

X = a person who lives in the wild and has no contact with civilization or written education and math at all.

Y = a person who got written education and math and then applied the remedy the full measure.

Mentally X is in the same state of mind as Y but the difference is Y is in civilization and in turn can communicate with the scribes, civilization, much easier than X can.

[Daniel 1:6 Now among these were of the children of Judah, Daniel, Hananiah, Mishael, and Azariah:]

This tribe was attacked by the scribes under the guidance of Nebuchadnezzar king of Babylon and the tribes have their most valued treasure, the arks of the covenant named : Daniel, Hananiah, Mishael, and Azariah taken. So Daniel is one of the arks and he is recording the event and that proves Daniel can write and that proves he got the education and since he is an ark it proves he applied the remedy the full measure. There are certainly some comments out of sequence which shows the right brain random access aspect was factoring into the texts. Reading, writing and math is a tool and after one gets that they are mentally hindered but they still have the tool but then if one applies the remedy the full measure they have the tool and they have this holy spirit third mind aspect going for them and they are godlike in intelligence in contrast to a person who just got the education and did not apply the remedy. I have no tolerance for mentally hindering human beings and robbing them of their third mind aspect and so I have no tolerance for beings that give human beings this education and then do not suggest the remedy to them so you can quote me when I say I have no tolerance. That's a nice way of saying do not ever think I have tolerance relative to this situation. If you think there is tolerance when it comes to mentally hindering infinitely wise beings and leaving them in a mental state of retardation, robbed of the "third mind" aspect that is only because you are delusional. Coveting the past suggests dreading the future.

[Luke 17:33 Whosoever(scribe) shall seek to save his life(mindfully, when the shadow of death arrives) shall lose it(stay in hell; mentally hindered); and whosoever(scribe) shall lose his life (mindfully; lets go when the shadow of death arrives) shall preserve it(escape hell and return to God graces, restore the third mind aspect).]

Lord: a person who has authority, control, or power over others; a master, chief, or ruler. = Authority = [Mark 1:22 And they were astonished at his doctrine: for he taught them as one that had authority, and not as the scribes.]

At this time period of Jesus we have some major scribe players.

Herod was the religious authority; chief priest scribe. Pontius Pilate was the government authority scribe.

Jesus had applied the remedy and achieved the holy spirit third mind aspect using John the Baptists water version of the remedy. Holding ones head under water will get the hypothalamus to give a fight or flight signal although it is somewhat risky to apply the remedy that way.

[Mark 1:10 And straightway coming up out of the water, he saw the heavens opened, and the Spirit like a dove descending upon him:]

Heavens opened up means he restored this third mind aspect after applying the remedy so he was [skilful in all wisdom]. or "all knowing."

So Jesus spoke and the common people determined this :

[Mark 1:22 And they were astonished at his doctrine: for he taught them as one that had authority, and not as the scribes(chief priest scribes and government authority scribes; official scribe authorities).]

As the reputation of Jesus increased it got back to the "official" authorities(scribes) and they determined this.

[Mark 11:18 And the scribes (Pontius Pilate) and chief priests (Herod) heard it, and sought how they might destroy him: for they feared him, because all the people was astonished at his doctrine.]

Why did the official authorities [feared him]? Because he achieved this Holy spirit state of mind and so he was [skilful in all wisdom] and the common people started thinking "Why is Herod and Pontius Pilate our rulers when clearly Jesus is wiser than they are in all areas?" This is why the official authorities had to find a way to get rid of Jesus because simply put, a person of sound mind or a person that achieves the perfect lateralization and achieves this third mind aspect is more intelligent by leaps and bounds than a scribe or a person who gets the education and does not apply the remedy simply because of this reality:

"When the brain is whole, the unified consciousness of the left and right hemispheres adds up to more than

the individual properties of the separate hemispheres."
- Roger Sperry

A side note: Some animals have very tiny brains but because of the lateralization or unified aspect, getting more than the sum of the two hemispheres, third mind aspect, they appear quite clever.

So Jesus was all knowing or skillful in all wisdom and he gave a contrast to the common people and the common people started saying "Why do we have these two retard official scribe rulers ruling us when we could have Jesus ruling us?" Simply put, if you went to work tomorrow and you were the president of your company and a new guy started that day and he was in a meeting and he said things in that meeting that made you look like an idiot relative to understanding the business, people in your company would start to question why you are the president of the company at all, and then perhaps jealously, envy and your pride might be hurt and before you know it you may hate that new guy who always makes you look stupid at the business meetings in front of all the employee that are below you in authority. This concept is what happened and is what this comment means:

[Mark 11:18 And the scribes(Pontius Pilate) and chief priests(Herod) heard it, and sought how they might destroy him: for they feared him, because all the people was astonished at his doctrine.]

[feared him] Is a clue; relative to 2Timothy 1:7.

[2 Timothy 1:7 For God hath not given us the spirit of fear; but of power, and of love, and of a sound mind.]

Fear is a symptom of an unsound mind and proof these beings had not applied the remedy. Another way to look at it is, certainly Herod and Pilate knew math, they had to count their money, and knew how to read and write yet they also had fear, so they had not applied the remedy.

Jesus was not slightly wiser than Pontius Pilate and Herod and all their friends combined he was infinitely wiser than Pontius Pilate and Herod and all their friends combined because this third mind aspect created when the mind is in perfect harmony means ones cerebral ability is multiplied by leaps and bounds in contrast to a person who does not that have third mind aspect simply because that third mind aspect is greater than the sum of the two hemisphere parts.

This : [unified consciousness of the left and right hemispheres adds up to more than the individual properties of the separate hemispheres.] = [adds up to more]

What it adds up to is not measurable or nameable in power, one becomes all knowing or skillful in all wisdom. So Jesus was not good at understanding ethics, law, economics, politics, science, medicine, teaching and any other topic one can come up with relative to that time period he was a Lord above all Lords, he applied the remedy well, in all of those areas and these "officials" were only good at their little narrow area of expertise and so they looked like fools in contrast to Jesus and so they had to get rid of him quickly or they would be out of power. Jesus in principle was similar to Solomon, he was just very wise even in contrast to the very wise and the common people (scribes) want a wise ruler and so the official rulers control was in jeopardy. If one wanted the best man for the job they would pick Jesus and the official rulers relative to religious and government aspects did not like that idea so they had to find a way to kill him.

[and sought how they might destroy him: for they feared him,]

They did not fear Jesus as much as they feared they would be out of power if he was allowed to continue to speak. The official rulers saw their power was fading every time Jesus spoke to the common people and that is an indication of how intelligent one becomes when they apply the remedy and achieve this perfect mental lateralization and thus achieve this third mind aspect the ancient texts call "Filled with the Holy Spirit". The deeper reality is any scribe that applies the remedy the full measure will be this: [skilful in all wisdom] and that perhaps is infinitely bad news to a control structure. You cannot scam a person that is skillful in all wisdom. You cannot pull a fast one on a person that is skillful in all wisdom. You cannot trick a person that is skillful in all wisdom. You cannot manipulate a person that is skillful in all wisdom, yet a control structure relies on being able to do that. The scribes relative to this story only had one choice, kill Jesus or they would lose their control. Another way to look at it is Jesus was not only skillful in all wisdom and a threat to the control structure he also was telling the common people how they could apply the remedy, "those who lose their life (mindfully) preserve it", and so the control structure saw maybe there would be lots of beings similar to Jesus' wisdom level, (filled with the Holy Spirit) if Jesus was allowed to continue to speak to the common people. In one way Jesus was telling the common people "Here is how you can be skillful in all wisdom and then you do not need a control structure that extorts money out of you, takes advantage of you and makes slaves out of you." So this suggests a hint that perhaps the education is a method to keep everyone from being skillful in all wisdom and thus makes them easy to manipulate and taken advantage of; easy to "herd" like little blind sheep. That's not going to go over well.

A deeper reality is a scribe or person that has not applied the remedy may think that once they apply the remedy they will have all this control and power potential over others but once the remedy is applied they return to sound mind or mental harmony and in that state of mind one is not prone to control or one does not lust to covet. One way to look at it is if any of the wise beings in the ancient texts were looking to take advantage of their mental clarity over others they would not have suggested the remedy and given away that secret freely.

[Luke 17:33 .; and whosoever shall lose his life (mindfully) shall preserve it.]

[Psalms 23:4 Yea, though I walk through the valley of the shadow of death, I will fear no evil(submit):]

They give away the secret to why they are skillful in all wisdom so they give the remedy away freely so they are not holding it over anyone's head and that is logical because they are without aspects like greed or coveting. Let's say a company makes an invention and so they will protect that information so they will have a monopoly on that invention and then they can "hold it over others head" and that is the reverse of the what the wise beings in the ancient texts did. The ancient texts are written by these beings that are skillful in all wisdom and they had this remedy so anyone could be skillful in all wisdom and they could have made lots of money with that remedy but instead they gave the remedy away for free because they were not greedy and they did not covet or control the remedy because those aspects are not symptoms of a being in mental harmony or are not symptoms of a sound mind. Another way to look at it is the wise beings natural inclination was to give a most valuable secret, the remedy to the tree of knowledge, away freely. It cost many of them their life to give freely. Giving freely goes against the premise of an economic system so it is a bad trend to set relatively speaking. This is why in society beings that give freely or beings that are charitable are given awards and given medals and attention as if giving freely in a universe that gives us everything for free is special or unique.

The beings in the ancient texts gave the species the remedy to the tree of knowledge so all human beings could return to what all human beings are suppose to be and that is skillful in all wisdom, all knowing. Of course applying the remedy to the full measure is no walk in the park, psychologically speaking.

Taxes tend to be encouraged for safety, security and protection reasons and that is why they are forms of extortion and blackmail using fear tactics.

[Luke 2:1 And it came to pass in those days, that there went out a decree from Caesar Augustus, that all the world should be taxed.] = The control structure, ruler scribes, Caesar Augustus, decreed the world should be extorted or blackmailed and said decree has never been lifted because the world is now full of timid blind beings who easily fall for extortion tactics. As timidity or fear increases probability of being extorted or black mailed increases. The tyrant wants you to understand every text in the universe except these ancient texts. The tyrant will fill your head with every stupidity text in the universe to keep you from understanding what the ancient texts are saying. The tyrant will tell you the ancient texts are speaking about fairy tale pixie dust but will never suggest they are suggesting how the slavery of the species was achieved and the tyrant will do it unknowingly. The tyrant knows as your awareness and comprehension increases his control and probability of extorting you decreases. A tyrant sees slavery as peace and freedom as danger. One is only as free as their fear and timidity allows them to be. Timidity about cages is a proper fear. It is probable the music you like sucks just as bad as the music you dislike. Sex is relative to physical attraction as emotions are relative to mental distraction.

5/19/10 11:29 AM - There is a comments that says "A jack of all trades is a master of none."

The word "none" in that comment refers to nothingness or the machine state or being in the now so the comment is saying a person who is good at all trades is in nothingness and a master; trades being areas of wisdom but not exclusively. So the comment means a being that has applied the remedy the full measure tends to be a master of all trades, skillful in all wisdom, all knowing. The scribes assume that comment is saying: A person that knows to much does not know anything well. They take that comment on face value and never consider its deeper message. Of course "trades" is relative. I am not a master of "keeping the remedy a secret" trade.

[Daniel 1:7 Unto whom the prince of the eunuchs gave names: for he gave unto Daniel the name of Belteshazzar; and to Hananiah, of Shadrach; and to Mishael, of Meshach; and to Azariah, of Abednego.]

The English word eunuch is from the Greek eune ("bed") and ekhein ("to keep"), effectively "bed keeper". So the scribes bed keeper gave the captured four Arks new names. This comment is suggesting a concept where a person captures something or someone or takes control of something and names it. The concept

163

could be applied to a person who gets a new pet and they name it to suggest they own that pet. A person might get a new car and they might name it to suggest ownership. One example is the indigenous tribes of America are called Native Americans yet they are not really Americans that is just the name the scribes who captured them and control them call them. That's not going to go over well.

[Daniel 1:8 But Daniel purposed in his heart that he would not defile himself with the portion of the king's meat, nor with the wine which he drank: therefore he requested of the prince of the eunuchs that he might not defile himself.]

Daniel is suggesting he will not associate with the King of the scribes. It is like a person that is captured by the enemy and they refuse the enemies luxuries when they are offered. This scribe king is trying to perhaps manipulate, gain favor with these four Arks and Daniel suggests he did not take up the food offer so perhaps the other three did. [he might not defile himself.] This is suggesting Daniel is not going to consort with the enemy or be friends with the adversary. Another way to look at it is this Scribe king takes these four Arks hostage and then tries to be friends with them and Daniel says "No way I would rather starve to death so keep your food. Give me liberty or give me death." = [he would not defile himself with the portion of the king's meat, nor with the wine which he drank:]

[Daniel 1:9 Now God had brought Daniel into favour and tender love with the prince of the eunuchs.]

This is suggesting the bed keeper which may actually be a bit more complex than just a bed keeper perhaps is a go between relative to the king and these four Arks, is taking a liking to Daniel. This is kind of like a situation where a prison guard befriends a prisoner but this eunuchs is also a spy for the scribe king as well.

[Daniel 1:10 And the prince of the eunuchs said unto Daniel, I fear my lord the king, who hath appointed your meat and your drink: for why should he see your faces worse liking than the children which are of your sort? then shall ye make me endanger my head to the king.]

This "keeper" is attempting to explain to Daniel if anything happens to them, like they do not eat and they get sick he is going to get in trouble. This is suggesting these four "arks" are very valuable and so this "keeper" is saying my head is on the line if anything happens to you guys; [he see your faces worse liking] = if you get sick from not eating, so the keeper is saying please eat something for my sake. So this story so far is not supernatural it is simply talking about a trend, the scribes take advantage of the tribes "arks' they have captured, and hold them captive and that is the nature of beings in extreme left brain state caused by the education, they covet and control everything. So these four captive "arks" are going on a hunger strike and then they suggest they will eat and drink.

[Daniel 1:11 Then said Daniel to Melzar, whom the prince of the eunuchs had set over Daniel, Hananiah, Mishael, and Azariah,

Daniel 1:12 Prove thy servants, I beseech thee, ten days; and let them give us pulse to eat, and water to drink.

Daniel 1:13 Then let our countenances be looked upon before thee, and the countenance of the children that eat of the portion of the king's meat: and as thou seest, deal with thy servants.

Daniel 1:14 So he consented to them in this matter, and proved them ten days.

Daniel 1:15 And at the end of ten days their countenances appeared fairer and fatter in flesh than all the children which did eat the portion of the king's meat.

Daniel 1:16 Thus Melzar took away the portion of their meat, and the wine that they should drink; and gave them pulse.]

The arks decided to eat. It appears relatively speaking this scribe king is looking to get some information out of these arks and perhaps the remedy itself. They say the word children but that means the children of god, which is simply a person that gets the education has the god image in man veiled, right hemisphere, and then applies the remedy and returns to how they were mentally as a child, sound minded. There is no mention to what these four "arks" did wrong because they didn't do anything wrong they are just being controlled by the scribes kind of like a treasure. These "arks" are like aliens to the scribes because they are "skillful in all wisdom" so they are valuable to the scribes and this is an indication of how hard it is to apply the remedy the full measure. If one cuts right down to the core of the full measure remedy it goes something like this. One has to consciously want to literally die, then they have to consciously seek a situation where their mind says "you will die" then they have to consciously say when that happens "I do not care if I die." and that is what the word "meek" means. So the only people that would ever potentially be in that situation are the depressed and suicidal and because it is perceived to be seeking literal death and it's risky. It is only harsh because the damage caused by the education is harsh. It is perhaps just like chemotherapy. One has to nearly die, go right up to the edge of death and then somehow not die and that's the cure. Laughter is the best medicine for the curse but the remedy is the only cure. If one wants to look at it from a supernatural point of view, it is simply the tree put that serpent on ones back and that serpent is not an idiot and so to trick that serpent to get off ones back one has to trick that serpent into thinking the person has died, but the person does not literally die they pretend they are seeking to die and when death arrives they submit to it, and that tricks the serpent to let them go. That is the no details explanation of the remedy. One has to trick "it" into thinking they have died and then "it" leaves them alone and until that happens "it" will not leave them alone. That is the price one has to pay when they eat off the tree of knowledge. The remedy separates the wheat scribes from the chaff scribes.

[Daniel 1:17 As for these four children, God gave them knowledge and skill in all learning and wisdom: and Daniel had understanding in all visions and dreams.]

[these four children] = four arks ; four children of god; four that applied the remedy.

[God gave them knowledge and skill in all learning and wisdom:] Why? Because they applied the remedy and unveiled right hemisphere and achieved perfect mental lateralization and achieved the "Holy Spirit" or third mind aspect.

[and Daniel had understanding in all visions and dreams.] This is suggesting Daniel had some extra abilities perhaps above the other three arks or maybe not extra abilities but simply he was perhaps a Master in this area [understanding in all visions and dreams.] and the others were not as proficient but perhaps had aspects Daniel was not as proficient at.

[Daniel 1:18 Now at the end of the days that the king had said he should bring them in, then the prince of the eunuchs brought them in before Nebuchadnezzar.]

So eventually this scribe king wants to have a look at the "arks" he captured and is controlling but he is a scribe so he perhaps cannot really understand what they are saying, he perhaps hears but does not understand, and so he may just assume they are fools or crazy. The logic is a King is not crazy so if a king cannot understand someone with less "authority" than a king

168

then it must be that persons fault because it cannot be the king's fault because the king is understood to be "wise" or he wouldn't be a king, so to speak.

[Daniel 1:19 And the king communed with them; and among them all was found none like Daniel, Hananiah, Mishael, and Azariah: therefore stood they before the king.]

This line is out of sequence [therefore stood they before the king.] and is a signpost of authenticity. Proper sequence would be [therefore they stood before the king.]. This verse is suggesting how valuable these four arks are to the king. It is saying the king did not know of any beings as wise as these four beings. These arks are so valuable because they can explain the remedy if they wish so anyone who applies the remedy becomes an ark. The arks are "self replicating" so to speak. Your language is infinitely flawed. The arks can make more of their self is another way to look at it. The arks are all knowing or skillful in all wisdom so they are superior in contrast to the scribe who is mentally hindered so a scribe cannot really understand them or relate to them so then the arks become a kind of collector's item to the scribes; a focal point of idolatry. That is why the scribes kept these arks in captivity mostly because the scribes couldn't apply the remedy the full measure and become an ark perhaps, so the next best thing was to own an ark and in this case own four of them. The story is whoever has the ark has all power or extreme power or unlimited power and that is true because the arks are skillful in all wisdom so whoever owns one or controls one has an advantage over every other scribe. This is why the "bed keeper" had to make sure the arks kept eating to stay healthy, to have a good "pulse". The arks are not really concerned about health because that would denote ego, they are free spirits so to speak. One way to look at it is the arks are already skillful in all wisdom so they do not really have a purpose or have this craving to make sure they live as long as they can. The arks are wise enough to understand many cannot apply the remedy anyway which means the tree of knowledge is essentially fatal to most. The arks are at peace with what will happen because they already know what will happen, so to speak, they are all knowing. All human beings are all knowing unless they get the tree of knowledge and then they have to apply the remedy the full measure to return to that mental state. Skillful in all wisdom = all knowing. One might suggest to turn an all knowing being into a mental joke via the education conditioning and then leave them that way is a crime above all crimes.

[Daniel 1:20 And in all matters of wisdom and understanding, that the king enquired of them, he found them ten times better than all the magicians and astrologers that were in all his realm.]

So this attack on the tribes was not about land or money it was about this Scribe King capturing the arks, four arks and so this scribe king was very powerful then. Any one of these arks by their self was [ten times better than all the magicians and astrologers that were in all his realm.] Ten times better than all the other "wise"

170

scribes in this Kings domain. Not ten times better than one advisor the king had, ten times better than all the advisors combined. Daniel is telling the truth but he is avoiding saying "I was wiser than all the kings advisors combined. I was ten time wiser than all of the kings advisors."

"When the brain is whole, the unified consciousness of the left and right hemispheres adds up to more than the individual properties of the separate hemispheres." - Roger Sperry

What adds up to more than the individual properties of the separate hemispheres? The Holy Spirit or third mind aspect.

What is required for that third mind aspect to happen? unification or a perfect lateralization of the mind.

What would throw the mind out of this perfect lateralization and thus negate the chances of this third mind aspect happening? [reading, writing and arithmetic -- the domain and strength of the left brain.]

Daniel and the other arks had this "third mind" aspect and the scribes the king had as advisors did not so it was a no contest.

[Daniel 1:21 And Daniel continued even unto the first year of king Cyrus.]

So Daniel and these other arks were captive and used because they were skillful in all wisdom so their wisdom was a commodity that the king used to control his city or domain. Another way to look at it is the arks are not looking to control anyone because they know everything already and control suggests future expectations. Coveting is suggesting by controlling something one is better or stronger than if they are not controlling that thing or aspect. A king controls a city or a domain just like a leader controls a city or domain and that gives him a feeling of power but if one is all knowing there is no logic in controlling anything. The arks power is they are all knowing and skillful in all wisdom so it is not logical they would seek to control material aspects like people, land, money, for example. So this first chapter of Daniel is explaining a very simple concept. The scribe king sought to capture these very wise beings to give him an advantage because these wise beings were very good advisors so they were valuable to a king. The deeper reality is the king could have just applied the remedy the full measure and become one of these arks or vessels. I did not detect the arks suggest the remedy yet to the king though.

Written Education: A man made linear based tool encompassing reading, writing and mathematics that favors left hemisphere to the degree it hinders the beings mind essentially permanently because mastering the linear based inventions and maintaining mastery in said inventions creates an imbalance relative the unified consciousness of the left and right hemispheres and eliminates the possibility of the third mind aspect which adds up to more than the individual properties of the separate hemispheres.

X = left hemisphere traits, the weaker of the two hemisphere traits. No intuition, complexity or lightning fast random access processing. Roger Sperry explained quite clearly and correctly the two hemisphere traits are hardwired; so there is no way to get intuition out of the left hemisphere, for example.

Y = right hemisphere traits; reduced to a subconscious state by the written education.

Z = Third mind aspect, power is greater than the sum of both hemispheres.

So it appears one gets the education and their right brain traits are veiled so they are less than perfect mentally, perfect is relative to not lacking anything essential and one might assume that is not so bad but the deeper reality is not only is one less than perfect mentally they cannot achieve this third mind aspect. Other words, some people have more right brain traits apparent than others but they still do not have the third mind aspect because that requires unified lateralization or perfect mental harmony. So one is mentally hindered by the education because they have right brain traits veiled, then one is mentally hindered again because the education eliminates the possibility the unified lateralization aspect so the third mind aspect cannot be achieved unless they apply the remedy the full measure.

So this means the education mentally hinders a being on two levels. Because the left hemisphere has the lesser traits of the two hemispheres it means one could not be mentally hindered any more than the education hinders them but then they are also robbed of the third mind aspect at the same time so it is a double robbery.

5/20/10 3:04 PM - The story surrounding Mohammed is so valuable because it is more of an observation relative to how he found God and less of a miraculous conception, miraculous karma and fate and destiny situation, it is more of an observation so it is simply stating how he found God and leaving those details in because the observer is not as interested in determining what the details mean and more concerned with keeping an accurate record of the observation. So one can look at Moses and the story goes it was a miracle so to speak that the Queen found Moses floating down the river. It was a miracle so to speak Elizabeth, John the Baptists mother had John the Baptist because she was sterile because of her age. It was a miracle Mary had Jesus because she was a virgin. Then we have Mohammed and this is a detail about Mohammed [Discontented with life in Mecca, he retreated to a cave in the surrounding mountains for meditation and reflection.]
Mohammed was a merchant and a shepherd before he became discontented. One has to be good at math to be a merchant and in fact being a merchant is all about math. If one does not know math they will buy high and sell low and give incorrect change in the merchant business. Nearly all businesses outside of creative jobs like artist jobs are all about math. What that means is

the better you are at math the more you have favored your left hemisphere.

So this comment about Mohammed : [Discontented with life in Mecca, he retreated to a cave in the surrounding mountains for meditation   and reflection.] ; could be looked at like, since Mohammed was a merchant which requires lots of math skills he eventually became depressed or discontented with life, in Mecca, and went to a cave to meditate or reflect or isolate himself from society, the scribes. The point is perhaps Mohammed did not go to that cave to seek the shadow of death and fear not, and he did not go to that cave to lose his life mindfully to preserve it and he did not go to that cave to deny himself even though that is exactly what he ended up doing. Relative to Mohammed's perception this is perhaps why he went to that cave: [Discontented with life in Mecca, he retreated to a cave in the surrounding mountains for meditation   and reflection.] He was depressed so he went to a cave to isolate himself from the life he had become discontented with. He became discontented with society and the ways of society and the ways of the world of society. Mohammed was thinking perhaps "This cannot be all there is in life" and that is why he was discontented or depressed with the life he had seen so he was in a state of mental humility or meekness. The concept that one becomes depressed when they observe the world of the scribes or the world of society and sometimes they isolate their self from society happens all the time. So relative to six billion people on the planet there are many who are in this state of meekness or humility except society, the scribes, call them depressed or suicidal because these

175

beings tend to isolate there self from society and so the scribes determine these humble or meek beings need fixing with pills.

[Discontented with life] = relative to the scribes is depression or a suicidal state. The depression aspect is not rare but applying the remedy once in that meek or depressed state is rare. Often a depressed person will seek some sort of "drug" so they are not so depressed anymore and this could be antidepressants, recreational drugs, food or a creative outlet or a combination of those. This depressed state of mind is not what it appears to be. A person may say "I know someone who is depressed or suicidal" so relative to their observations they see a depressed person but that is not what that person is, in fact that person is doing this: [meditation and reflection.] A depressed person is attempting to mentally get their self out of the sense of time perception dimension the traditional education has put them in but they simply are not aware of that consciously because the traditional education has hindered their mind and thus their cognitive ability and thus their awareness and perception. Another way to look at it is a depressed person has their right brain intuition veiled so they are not aware of why they are depressed. The depressed person may say "I am depressed because I lost my job." or they may say "I am depressed because I am [discontented with life]" So a depressed person is a person that got the traditional education in one form or another or associated with beings that got the education and started to learn to read, write or do math and in doing that it veiled their right hemisphere and the depression is a symptom they are attempting to unknowingly undo that mental hindering. A depressed person may never perceive that is what is happening because their right brain aspects like intuition are veiled so they are "blind" or they do not have access to all their mental aspects so they cannot make proper observations relative to why they are depressed. Of course any being that got the traditional education or associated with beings that did have some aspects of their right hemisphere veiled so they cannot make proper observations either. Another way to look at it is a depressed scribe is making more accurate observations relative to what is going on than a happy scribe because they are starting to observe properly and thus they become [discontented with life]. These depressed beings are observing this life in the world of the scribes as disenchanting and they are right and so they become depressed so they are becoming aware of what is going on around them but they are still mentally hindered so the signals come out in very strange ways sometimes even backwards. Sometimes a depressed person sees their self as the problem. A depressed scribe is meek because they see their self as the problem. A scribe will suggest a suicidal scribe is selfish or seeking attention but in reality a suicidal scribe is self less which means they see their self as having no value. A suicidal scribe sees their self as the problem and not the world of the scribes. A suicidal scribe does not want to attack society they want to attack their self so they see their self as the problem and this is what deny yourself is in concept. A suicidal scribe is not looking at the log in the world of the scribe's eye they are looking at the infinite log in their eye and often they determine it is too large so they opt out of life so to speak and that is the trend of the suicidal scribe. This indicates the damage caused by the traditional education tends to be fatal in scribes that attempt to undo that damage unknowingly which is what a depressed scribe is doing. The trend is a scribe will never fully regain their mind after all the education taught to them as a child which means it is exceptional if a being does undo that damage fully and that is what the parable of sower is suggesting. Said parable is explaining there are many ways a scribe will not undo that mental damage and there is one way they can but it is exceptional if they do go that way. Because the education puts one mentally in an alternate perception dimension it is exceptional if a being can get their self out of that alternate perception dimension simply because the trend is a scribe will go with the flow of their perception and the remedy is one has to deny their perception or go against it. If one is in a spooky location at night alone with no lights and their mind says "Run like the wind" in order to deny that one has to yield to that perception or deny that perception or ignore that perception. The world of the scribes will suggest "Always trust your instincts" but the remedy suggests do not trust your instincts meaning deny your instincts relative to applying the remedy. That's a good example of the reverse thing and an indication of two alternate perception dimensions. Once one applies the remedy they can trust their instincts but after the education one has to deny their instincts so it is a true double standard and there is only one way to know if one has applied the remedy the full measure and that is no sense of time. Once one applies the remedy the full measure, about thirty days later relative to a calendar that beings entire perception shifts to the reverse pole of where they are at and so it is not subtle unless your definition of subtle is getting hit by a Mac Truck. So the remedy creates a complete and absolute polar shift relative to perception so one will go from sense of time perception dimension to no sense of time perception dimension in one second. One will have an "ah ha" sensation that never stops from then on out. There is nothing subtle about it. If one has a sense of time they have not applied the remedy because sense of time proves to one their right brain paradox aspect is veiled from their perception and so they need to apply the remedy to restore this perfect mental harmony which allows this "third mind" aspect to be achieved. There are perhaps no exceptions and that indicates that is perhaps an absolute. The polar shift relative to perception is so profound one will assume something horrible has happened. It is logical because a person has been in the sense of time perception dimension so long they see that as normal and then when they go to the no sense of time perception dimension and it is such a major change they assume it is abnormal and that is the moment the reverse aspect comes into focus. One becomes very aware of this reverse thing. That is to say in concept, what one thought was truth was not truth, what one thought was good was not good, what one thought was justice was not justice and this is an indication of a complete polar shift in perception. Another way to look at it is all illusions are revealed but the being needs some warming up time in order to fully grasp all the illusions. The moment the person loses their sense of time the right brain intuition is restored and this third mind aspect is achieved and that being is aware cerebrally of everything but only in concept which means they need a period of time perhaps over a year to catch up to what their intuition already knows or is aware of. So the concept of born again is very accurate because it means one applies the remedy and then the polar shift relative to perception happens and then the person has to relearn everything over again. One could look at it like a person finds out the number 2 really is the number 4 and so they have to redo all their calculations over. One has all these calculations or understandings they have had since they were young and now they find out the number 2 is really the number 4 and so they have to redo or recalculate every understanding they have had since they were young but that catch is, once this third mind aspect is achieved it will not take very long relative to a calendar. One goes from left brain linear processing and then they apply the remedy and regain right brain random access processing and then their mind is unified and so they activate the third mind aspect that is greater than the sum of the two hemispheres parts so they achieve this processing power that perhaps defies measurement and logic. It is not logical if you take left hemisphere traits (50) and combine them with right hemisphere traits (50) you achieve this third mind aspect worth (200). One might suggest the 200 is really infinity, all knowing. One can look at the mainframe computers, the biggest ones in the world with all their processing power and all of their information and data and think about how much wisdom they must have but in reality they have not figured out an elementary cause effect relationships relative to what all the left brain favoring education does to the mind and so they are worthless. All the main frame computers in the universe tied together and all their hard drives connected together and their water cooling towers and they still do not have the slightest clue what the tree of knowledge is so all that processing power is still at the level of retardation in contrast to this third mind aspect of the human mind. Perhaps you can prove how that is not true. Perhaps we invented computers to make up for the fact our minds are all hindered by the education because I am certain no mainframe will ever surpass the power of this third mind aspect achieved when the hemispheres are in a unified state.

Punch this data into all the main frames on the planet and see what they come up with and you will find out they are simply grains of sand.

X = "What it comes down to is that modern society discriminates against the right hemisphere." - Roger Sperry (1973) Neurobiologist and Nobel Lauriat

Y = "In humans, the frontal lobe reaches full maturity around only after the 20s, marking the cognitive maturity associated with adulthood" - Giedd, Jay N. (october 1999). "Brain Development during childhood and adolescence: a longitudinal MRI study". Nature neuroscience 2 (10): 861-863.

Z = " If you reflect back upon our own educational training, we have been traditionally taught to master the 3 R's: reading, writing and arithmetic -- the domain and strength of the left brain" - The Pitek Group, LLC. Michael P. Pitek, III

See if all the main frames on the planet will conclude : Z + Y = X

The main frames are worthless because they cannot tell the species the education keeps mentally putting us all to sleep and the main frames also cannot even figure out what the remedy to that slumber is, so they cannot save us. The main frames can calculate numbers very fast but they cannot tell us we mentally destroy ourselves with our own invention on an industrial scale so what value do they have? Who cares if the machines can see other galaxies we cannot even see how we harm ourselves. As a species we have used this third mind aspect to invent a tool that has eliminated the third mind aspect achieved when the hemispheres are perfectly unified. The beings in the ancient texts knew the remedy to restore that third mind aspect thousands of years ago and all the mainframes on the planet combined still have not figured that out. Certainly there are mainframes with copies of the Torah, the New Testament and the Quran in them so why haven't these main frames figured out the remedy yet? The answer is they do not have the processing power that even compares the third mind processing power of the human mind and they perhaps never will. Computers do not have intuition and that single aspect is beyond measure in the third mind state. The pattern detection in the third mind state far exceeds anything a mainframe could ever achieve. Just these two aspects, pattern detection and intuition, in the third mind state are beyond measure relative to how powerful they are. The intuition aspect is not relative to telling a person what number they are thinking of, it is more along the lines of detecting a problem no scribe can see or detect. The intuition deals with the unseen yet seen cerebrally. Another way to look at it is the intuition separates the quick from the dead, the blind from those with sight. The intuition is in fact just like "eyes" but it sees what the eyes cannot see. The scribes will often say "Show me the proof" and that is because they do not understand human beings have senses that far exceed the elementary vision, hearing, taste and touch senses because these intuition and pattern detection senses were taken from them by the education starting when they were just children. This third mind aspect the ancient texts call the Holy Spirit or the spirit of God means we are "all knowing" in our mental capacity when this third mind aspect is restored and there perhaps may not be any difference between God like and God. Maybe you should call your scribe cult leader and ask him about that one. Maybe we are the most powerful life form in the universe which means looking for other life forms is perhaps quite vain. Maybe other life forms do not seek us out because they are aware we are the most powerful life form and just we don't know that because we tend to get lost in our own infinite understanding sometimes and make things that put us to sleep, like reading, writing and math. Perhaps we put our self to sleep because we are bored but it may mean the end of our spices if we do not wake our self up. Perhaps some of these concepts are hard to grasp until the third mind aspect is restored but a positive note is the concept of restoring the third mind aspect which is the remedy is easy to understand for anyone but making the decision to apply said remedy is perhaps the tricky part. Nothing is going to happened to you if you cannot apply the remedy so do not assume there is pressure on you because just reaching a mental state to understand the remedy in the sense of time perception dimension mental state is enough pressure as it is. The trend is a being that has been mentally conditioned for all those years of education cannot apply the remedy so the exception is one can, and that reality alone is more than enough of a burden for anyone to bear.

Computer communication is based on binary and that is numbers and the numbers are zero and one representing "off" and "on" and off and on are absolutes. So absolutes are relative to a number system and a number system is relative to computers. Quantum mechanics suggest probabilities which is contrary to absolutes. Left hemisphere deals with absolutes and right hemisphere deals with probabilities. One problem with absolutes is one must first determine exactly where the universe is before they can determine exactly where they are at.

5/20/10 8:39 PM -

Adam, Idris (Enoch), Nuh (Noah), Hud (Heber), Saleh (Shelah), Ibrahim (Abraham), Lut (Lot), Ismail (Ishmael), Ishaq (Isaac), Yaqub (Jacob), Yusuf

(Joseph), Shoaib (Jethro), Musa (Moses), Harun (Aaron), Davud (David), Suleyman (Solomon), Ayub (Job), Ilyas (Elias), Zulkifl (Ezekiel), Al-Yasa (Elisha), Yunus (Jonah), Zakariya (Zechariah), Yahya (John the Baptist), Isa (Jesus), Muhammad.

Five prophets are considered major: Nuh (Noah), Ibrahim (Abraham), Musa (Moses), Isa (Jesus), and Muhammad.

This is a list of Prophets relative to the western hemisphere which would be the middle east relative to the time period and the first pattern perhaps no one can argue with is all of these beings lived after the invention of Sumerian written language which was essentially 5400 years ago. It perhaps is important to understand the difference between a prophet and a disciple.

Prophet is the same thing as saying this: Sammasambuddhas attain buddhahood, then decide to teach others the truth they have discovered.

Disciple is the same thing as saying this: Paccekabuddhas, sometimes called "silent Buddhas" are similar to sammasambuddhas in that they attain nirvana and acquire many of the same powers as a sammasambuddha, but are unable to teach what they have discovered.

The difference between this :[decide to teach others the truth they have discovered.] and this [are unable to teach what they have discovered.] is fear and that is relative to this comment [Revelation 3:16 So then because thou art lukewarm, and neither cold nor hot, I will spue thee out of my mouth.]

A disciple is lukewarm, a prophet is hot, a scribe is cold. It is easier to look at it like the world of the scribes is a large company or corporation and they have lots of influence and lots of weapons and so the scribes can eliminate any problem that gets in their way quite easily. So a whistle blower is a worker in the corporation and they discover a truth about this corporation and decide to tell the world about that truth but they know that corporation will try to stop them and so the whistle blower must not be afraid at all because the cooperation does not play games with whistle blower's. The world of the scribes is Goliath so only the Prophets have no fear because they stand up to Goliath and the disciples attempt to say things like "Listen to what the prophets say, they are wise." For example the disciples of Jesus did not say "deny yourself" and they did not say "those who lose their life preserve it." Jesus said that , so the disciples wrote down those comments and said Listen to what Jesus said and do what Jesus said." because they were [unable to teach what they have discovered.] so they were reduced to saying "Do what Jesus taught." This gives off the impression the prophets are chosen or unique but that is perhaps an illusion, the reality is the remedy is very hard to apply the full measure. The prophets just so happen to have applied the remedy the full measure. This is perhaps an indication of how devastating the education is on the mind not an indication of being chosen. One way to look at it is, it is one thing to be in a spooky situation and your mind says "If you do not run there is a 90% chance you will die." and it is another thing to be in a spooky situation where your mind says "It is 100% chance you will die if you do not run." and if one applies the self control remedy in that latter state of mind one becomes a prophet or sammasambuddha. This comment is suggesting the prophets wanted everyone to apply the remedy the full measure, or hot: [Revelation 3:16 So then because thou art lukewarm, and neither cold nor hot, I will spue thee out of my mouth.] Only in applying the remedy the full measure which is hot will one fully restore the third aspect of their mind created when both hemisphere traits are unified which means in perfect harmony. There is a complexity where there are levels of sammasabuddha. Relative to the west these are the Lords of the Lords: Nuh (Noah), Ibrahim (Abraham), Musa (Moses), Isa (Jesus), and Muhammad but certainly for example the disciples may also have been at the level of sammasabuddha just not one the level of this "big fish". Simply put the disciples were "skillful in all wisdom" relative to all the scribes put together but the "big fish" were even wiser. Unnamable in cerebral power is what the "big fish" were and the disciples were just a bit under that level perhaps. The list of prophets is relative to the area of the world and relative to the known understandings at the time. Socrates said no true philosopher fears death and that is the remedy and in Buddhism the full measure remedy is to go to a cemetery at night alone and mediate, and those beings are not on the list but we all know for certain Socrates went up against the scribes because he was outspoken against written language when it came into being in Greece and that's why it was suggested Socrates corrupted the minds of the youth and by suggesting that to the youth he paid with his life.

Yunus (Jonah): He applied the remedy lukewarm , detected it was lukewarm and applied the remedy again the full measure: [Jonah 1:12 And he said unto them, Take me up, and cast me forth into the sea;] then he warmed up and went right to the King of the city and told him the situation and told the King the remedy and so he was a whistle blower and even after he achieved that he gave up because he knew knowing the full measure remedy and applying the full measure remedy is two totally different things and so Jonah knew tree of knowledge does too much damage. The probability one can apply the full measure remedy after getting the education is less than the probability civilization will question if written education harms the mind. The probability one can apply the full measure remedy after getting the education is less than the probability a person that gets the education will have the cognitive ability required to determine they need to apply the full measure remedy. This freewill concept plays multiple roles because firstly no sound minded being would by freewill choose to have their right hemisphere traits veiled so the third mind aspect is veiled so they in turn are far less aware or intelligent as they were when they were born but the world of the scribes has laws that say everyone has to get that done to them, so firstly freewill is not happening. After one gets the education one has to freely apply the remedy which means no one can force them to apply the remedy because it is a battle within their mind which means group efforts mean nothing perhaps. This comment does not say 'Let's all go throw ourselves into the sea" ; [Take me up, and cast me forth into the sea;] Jonah by freewill decided to have himself cast into the sea while the sea was rough in the middle of a storm and that is absolute submission and absolute deny one's self and absolute fear not because certainly Jonah's mind was telling him "If you have them throw you into the sea this far out in the middle of a storm you will certainly die." The fact he did not die shows one how delicate this remedy is, he could have just as well drowned. Chemotherapy takes one right to the edge of death and sometimes they are cured and sometimes they die and the remedy is the same thing relative to the full measure aspect of the remedy. That is the price one has to pay the piper if they wish to push extreme left brain linear tools on the delicate mind of a child and the sooner one faces that reality the sooner one will respect the education technology and not just throw it on people like it is flawless and can never harm anyone because it factually kills people. You may say you have never murdered anyone but I say you have been an accomplice in the factual murder of millions of children and the fact you are not aware of that only proves your an insane person killing children and are not even aware of it.

[J. C. (13) hung himself after allegedly being bullied at school.]

One cannot push all the left brain education on tiny children and then expect them not to emotionally implode when the slightest problem comes up but as Dante suggested the scribes head(mind) has been turned backwards and they cannot see one step in front of their self. You are what the scribes have sown so you have to be pulled up allowed to wither in the sun and then replanted in proper soil and some do not survive the "wither in the sun part".

It's all or nothing. All = scribes: Nothing = ones that apply the remedy; one in nothingness or the machine state.

[Ibrahim (Abraham)]
[Genesis 15:1 After these things the word of the LORD came unto Abram in a vision, saying, Fear not, Abram: I am thy shield, and thy exceeding great reward.]

This is the first suggestion of fear not which is the remedy and of course everyone knows the Abraham and Isaac story of sacrifice which is the fear not remedy concept being applied. Lot is in this list and he was with Abraham when they attacked the scribe's cities of Sodom and Gomorrah. Lot was Abraham brother's son and Abraham's brother's name was Haran. So this suggests Abraham may have also applied his remedy on Lot also as well as his own son Isaac, but Isaac was not at the attack of the scribes unless Isaac was considered in the two armies of "angels" and that suggests Lot applied the remedy rather well because he was a major player or mentioned oft in that battle.

Idris (Enoch)

[Genesis 5:24 And Enoch walked with God: and he was not; for God took him.]

[and he was not] = not relative to nothingness or in the now or one without ego and pride because ego and pride are relative to sense of time or relative to a person who has not applied the remedy; relative to this comment: [Galatians 5:2 Behold, I Paul say unto you, that if ye be circumcised, Christ shall profit you nothing.] = If you apply the remedy which is sacrifice you shall be rewarded with nothingness, the machine state. If you do as Jesus suggested and deny yourself the full measure your reward will be you achieve this third mind aspect called the Holy Spirit and be in infinity and that is nothingness or nothing. It is complex but one way to look at it is a person who is proud is a person who has prejudice because to suggest one is proud they have to also understand the opposite of proud which is shame, but a person in the machine state has no concept of either pride or shame because they are in nothingness or have no prejudice. So the word "circumcised" is what the remedy was called at the time of Abraham and also at the time of Jesus meaning cut or sacrificed. If one submits they sacrifice their self. If one denies their self they sacrifice their self. If one fears not when the shadow of death arrives they sacrifice their self. This of course is not a lifelong profession, applying the remedy, it is a one second mental self control decision made in the proper situation. The logic being relative to why women were not suggest to be "circumcised" is because males tended to get the reading writing and math not the women at this period in time. The very fact the scribes even today cut a small child's penis thinking it is going to do anything relative to apply this remedy is an indication of how out classed the scribes are relative to these texts. It is a simple concept; these texts were written by beings that were factually skillful in all wisdom and they did not take kindly to the scribes and what the scribes did to children so it is logical they would use code words knowing if the mentally hindered scribes read them they would assume it was literal and harm their self. Simply put the scribes are human beings that invented something that destroyed their mind and because their mind is destroyed they are unknowingly harming all the children and the beings in these texts are not playing games with them and the sooner you understand there are absolutely no rules and no quarter given ever in this battle the sooner you will understand one thing. You go ahead and keep cutting the innocent males penis when they are infants and tell yourself that is going to assist them in undoing twelve years of left brain favoring education conditioning they get later in life. There is no medical evidence a male circumcised has any benefits at all in fact there is suggestions it hinders the male sexual aspects relative to sensitivity so obviously the scribes misunderstood what that code word meant in the ancient texts. To put it in perspective Abraham suggested circumcise perhaps three or four thousand years ago and the scribes are still harming their own children as a result of that code word which simply means the fear not remedy which is sacrifice. This is a slight hint at who these beings in the ancient texts were relative to how wise and clever and how much foresight they had and is also an indication perhaps that they were never going to accept the scribes or be friends with the scribes or tolerate the deeds of the scribes relative to the mental hindering of the children. The fact that the scribes still publish the ancient texts and do not even perceive said texts mock them is certainly one of the greatest inside jokes in the history of the species.

[Hud (Heber)] : ["O my Hud! No evidence have you brought us, and we shall not leave our gods for your mere saying! And we are not believers in you. All that we say is that some of our gods (false deities) have seized you with evil (madness)." (Ch 11:53-54 Quran)]
Eber was Hud in the Torah so Mohammed was again speaking of the beings before him. The big fish easily detect the big fish one might suggest.

Hud was simply a being that applied the remedy and he spoke out against idolatry which is a symptom of a mind that covets. Idolatry is relative to greed, lust, pride, envy, jealousy, wrath and thus control and a mind that is sound has random access thoughts so none of these states of mind can really be achieved or maintained. The scribes said Hud was crazy [All that we say is that some of our gods (false deities) have seized you with evil (madness).]
This is a description of who Hud lived with [The people of 'Ad lived many years in the windswept hills of an area between Yemen and Oman. They were physically well built and renowned for their craftsmanship especially in the construction of tall buildings with lofty towers.

] and the key pattern here is [construction of tall buildings with lofty towers.] because math is required for architecture. One can contrast this statement: [All that we say is that some of our gods (false deities) have seized you with evil (madness).] with this statement [Mark 10:34 And they shall mock him, and shall scourge him, and shall spit upon him, and shall kill him: and the third day he shall rise again.] and this one [Job 21:3 Suffer me that I may speak; and after that I have spoken, mock on.]

Jobs comment is perhaps great humor. It is saying in spirit "Let me speak scribes and then you can mock me and tell yourself I am wrong because your hindered mind cannot grasp you simply don't have cognitive ability to understand me any longer after all that education."

[Luke 23:10 And the chief priests and scribes stood and vehemently accused him.] = [All that we say is that some of our gods (false deities) have seized you with evil (madness).]

[Matthew 9:3 And, behold, certain of the scribes said within themselves, This man blasphemeth.] = [All that we say is that some of our gods (false deities) have seized you with evil (madness).]

The deeper reality is the education alters ones perception and so a person that applies the remedy is in another perception dimension attempting to talk scribes in the sense of time perception dimension into applying the remedy to get out of that alternate perception dimension the education has put them in but the scribes have a greatly hindered cognitive ability in that sense of time perception dimension so they often perceive sanity as insanity or madness. Another way to look at it is; it is probable an insane person will see sanity as insanity. So one has to have a test to see which of these beings are really insane. The easiest test relative to the current time period is: Is it possible or impossible all the linear based education may have mentally unwanted side effects on the mind of a child? It is understood all of civilization perceives the correct answer is: it is impossible.

Modern civilization or society has to perceive it is impossible because if they considered it was possible the education may hinder children then they also have to submit it is possible they are mentally hindering children on an industrial scale and forcefully by law. My argument is it is probable all the left brain favoring education hinders the mind and I can testify to that because I was mentally hindered by it and the scribe's argument is, it is impossible you were hindered by it and you are crazy. If the scribes ever suggest anything less than "It is crazy to suggest written education and math hinders the mind of children" they are in hot water.

Hud is first mentioned in the Torah and then mentioned again in the New Testament, Luke 3:35. It was suggested he was a merchant and that is another pattern relative to math. So Hud being mentioned in all three main religious texts in the west suggests the Torah, The New Testaments and the Quran are not three separate books they are in fact one book simply written over the span

195

of thousands of years and are testimonies of human beings who applied the remedy well. So there are these three religions created from these three texts and the reason for that is the scribes are in this extreme left brain state because they have not applied the remedy and a left brain trait is seeing parts. The scribes see three separate books and so they created three separate religions but once one applies the remedy they see these three books are one large book and suggest one principle core problem, the mental effects of written education, and the one principle core remedy to that one core problem. One of Mohammed's last words were "We the community of Prophets are not inherited. Whatever we leave is for charity." Who is the community of prophets? Everyone on the above list and also some others but the list is very small relative to how many human beings get this education and do not apply the remedy the full measure. All of these being lived in civilization or were raised in civilization so they were exposed or had contact with the scribes and then they applied the remedy the full measure and then spoke out against the scribes which is civilization but they were not on an absolute scale against civilization they simply were attempting to suggest there were some problems with civilizations golden calf, reading writing and math and the scribes even today as a whole simply cannot grasp that because in part relative to their perception the problems that would have to be faced if civilization as a whole suggested there may be problems with the education would create a backlash where the scribes or civilization or the control structure would perhaps never be trusted again.

[Whatever we leave is for charity.] This comment is suggesting in all of these texts is the remedy in one form or another and so as long as that remedy survives and is given away some beings may be able to apply it and that perhaps is as good as it gets. So these three texts explain the remedy, the reason for the remedy, the conflict with the scribes and then testimonies of beings that have applied the remedy. On that level the texts are one text. The scribes tend to get lost in the details and see these texts as all saying something different because they see many parts in that extreme left brain state caused by the education and of course the devil is in or is the details. The big fish always detect the other big fish and that will never change.

Yahya (John the Baptist):
[Mark 1:10 And straightway coming up out of the water, he saw the heavens opened, and the Spirit like a dove descending upon him:
Luke 3:21 Now when all the people were baptized, it came to pass, that Jesus also being baptized, and praying, the heaven was opened,
Luke 3:22 And the Holy Ghost descended in a bodily shape like a dove upon him, and a voice came from heaven, which said, Thou art my beloved Son; in thee I am well pleased.]

The spirit of this text is saying Jesus used or allowed John the Baptist to use his water version of the remedy, hold a person under water and when their hypothalamus says "Surface or you will drown" one denies their self or fears not or submits, and then Jesus achieved the "Holy Spirit" or third mind aspect. Then John the Baptist said "Thou art my beloved Son; in thee I am well pleased." which is simply a Master saying "You listened to my suggestion of the remedy and applied it very well and you did well for doing so." John is saying "You focused on the log in your eye and I am pleased with that." I am mindful certain beings will take issues with the suggestion that Jesus had to apply the remedy and those same beings will also suggest "those who lose their life(mindfully) will preserve it" is false also. That's a nice way of saying before any being starts suggesting what their scribe cult leader told them about any of these texts they perhaps should first apply the remedy because until they do they factually do not have the mental clarity or cognitive ability to understand what these texts are suggesting.

So John the Baptists father was Zacharias and this comment suggests he knew the remedy: [Luke 1:13 But the angel said unto him, Fear not, Zacharias: for thy prayer is heard; and thy wife Elisabeth shall bear thee a son, and thou shalt call his name John.] So it is logical Zacharias assisted his son with the remedy and then John the Baptist assisted others with the remedy and before the scribes cut his head off for "waking up" people with his version of the remedy one of those beings that woke up well by using the water version of the remedy John suggested or assisted with is Jesus. So there is no blood relations relative to John the Baptist and Jesus but they are bound by this remedy. So this suggests Zacharias started the New Testament "revival" so to speak, knowingly or unknowingly, probably knowingly. It is kind of like that commercial "they tell a friend" where Zacharias tells his son John the Baptist the remedy and then his son tells Jesus the remedy and Jesus tells his disciples the remedy and so on. So this remedy is what is referred to as the good news. The bad news is the reading, writing, and math aborts this Holy Spirit or third mind aspect all beings have and the good news is the remedy restores it.

[Luke 1:30 And the angel said unto her, Fear not, Mary: for thou hast found favour with God.] This is suggesting Mary also knew the remedy. One has to understand "fear not" is the code word for the remedy just as "circumcised" is also the code word for the remedy; sacrifice. So "fear not" is suggested with a person's name and that indicates that person understands the remedy and one pattern is it is followed by the person's name.

[Genesis 15:1 ..... Fear not, Abram: ...] Abram was Abraham's name before he applied the remedy. So the change of name is suggesting he is "born again" so one gets their new name, so to speak, but it is not an absolute it is just a detail. Some changed their name after applying the remedy and in the case of John the Baptist and Jesus for example some did not change their name after applying the remedy.

[Luke 1:13 But the angel said unto him, Fear not, Zacharias:..]

[Luke 1:30 And the angel said unto her, Fear not, Mary:]

One thing to notice is there is a ":" after the "fear not, name" suggestion in all three of these comments.
[Fear not, Abram:]
[Fear not, Zacharias:]
[Fear not, Mary:]

So it is saying in "code" or in spirit, Abram applied the fear not remedy, Zacharias applied the fear not remedy, Mary applied the fear not remedy. It is like a title or a code for explaining who one can trust. You know everything Abraham suggested was true because the remedy is in front of his name, for example. If one just substitutes the title "Master" for "fear not" it would be Master Abram, Master Zacharias, Master Mary. Because the remedy works on anyone who applies it, it is something that can be explained as having validity relative to the understandings of neurology relative to how the amygdala and the hypothalamus work in conjunction with each other. This may explain why Mary watched Jesus on the cross, because she was a female master and the scribes perhaps did not take much notice to her relative to her being a threat. The remedy works just as well on women as it does on males. Males and females both have a hypothalamus and have an amygdala so one applies the remedy and the amygdala remembers that and no longer allows the hypothalamus to send so many false fight or flight signals and so that concept applies to both sexes equally it just may be the case the women tended not to fight the scribes openly, verbally or physically, relative to the time of these texts.

So this remedy allowed this secret society within the confines of the scribe's society and it is logical codes would have to be used to keep it a secret. Some beings who attempted to go mainstream with the remedy were butchered by the scribes namely John the Baptist, Jesus and the disciples and that is logical because the scribes do not take kindly to people not only speaking poorly of their golden calf, reading, writing and math, but on top of that these beings could also assist scribes to apply the remedy in various ways and then those scribes "saw the light" and joined the "secret society" of the ones who spoke out against the golden calf. It is one thing to suggest reading, writing and math hinders the mind, it is another thing to suggest how any being who got said education can apply this remedy and find out for their self how much damage that education did to their mind. It is one thing to complain about something but it is another thing to complain about something and then offer the absolute solution to it backed up by thousands of years of written testimonies relative to the solutions validity. Be mindful if you insult any of these wise beings in any of the ancient texts you insult all of them because they are all [the community of Prophets]. Another way to look at it is these beings in the ancient texts were all speaking out about the problems with that god the scribes pray to and that god is Thoth and Thoth is associated with writing and literacy and everything that is relative to that. There are these stats the scribes keep that you know as literacy rates and they tout them as if they are some key to determining the intelligence level of a country or civilization. "the world literacy rate is low so we are in trouble" kind of thing. The trend is once a person gets all of this "literacy" they cannot undo the mental damage and restore the "third mind" aspect so for a scribe to go out and suggest "Everyone needs to be literate" is an absolute symptom of insanity which is essentially lack of foresight. The scribes will say "everyone needs to be literate" but they forget to mention "and once one is literate the third mind aspect is destroyed and only a handful of beings in the last 5000 years have ever fully undone that damage." Literate is relative to math also. A being with stage five cancer can put on nice clothes and smile and tell everyone everything is fine and pull it off. That is essentially what the ruler scribes of civilization do because all they ever are capable of suggesting are very superficial one step linear explanations for everything and it is not they perceive that is what they do it is simply after all that left brain favoring education that is all they are capable of doing until they apply the remedy the full measure and only a handful of beings in 5000 years have ever done that.

David (David): David stood up to the scribes, the ones that number like the grains in the sea.

[1 Samuel 18:6 And it came to pass as they came, when David was returned from the slaughter of the Philistine, that the women came out of all cities of Israel, singing and dancing, to meet king Saul, with tabrets, with joy, and with instruments of musick.

202

1 Samuel 18:7 And the women answered one another as they played, and said, Saul hath slain his thousands, and David his ten thousands.]

The women in these two comments were very happy. Why would the women be happy? Because the tools the scribes push on the children harm the children and destroy this "third mind" or "Holy Spirit" aspect and that is harming children and females do not take kindly to the offspring being harmed even though males in contrast are somewhat indifferent to it.

http://www.liveleak.com/view?i=6ef_1195194475

This is a video of a male lion killing the cubs and the females cannot stop it. So these females in the above verse are this [that the women came out of all cities of Israel, singing and dancing, to meet king Saul, with tabrets, with joy, and with instruments of musick.] because these females could count on David and Saul to protect the children from the scribes who were harming the "cubs". The women cannot fight physically against the scribe males is one way to look at it because that is not their nature. So the education made the males insane, the first scribes were males, and then they took over everything and that means they have a last say on the well being of the offspring and they decide the offspring are all going to get the education also, and at this point they even make sure all the females get it and so it is just a lunatic asylum. Civilization is not maybe a lunatic asylum because of this education it is an absolute mad house to the absolute degree. All of civilization takes six year old children and destroys those children's minds relative to the third mind aspect and then suggests they are wise and then suggests they seek all children should get the education, and then they never even suggest the education may have unwanted mental side effects and so they never suggest the remedy to the unwanted side effects and that is because they do not think the education has unwanted side effects because they do not have the cognitive ability because they got the education to reason and detect elementary cause and effect relationships relative to what all that left brain education will do to the delicate mind of a child. If a person is bragging about killing children which is factually what the education does to the mind and thus often to the person, and they perceive they are doing a good deed, they are insane. Our spices has inadvertently made itself insane with this left brain favoring invention and since we are insane we cannot even detect we are insane or what has made us insane. Since as a species our cognitive ability is compromised we do not have the cognitive ability to detect we have a compromised cognitive ability and we cannot detect what caused it. The blind leading the blind into blindness. I do not suggest one country is like that I suggest the entire boat is like that. When you find a single country in this narrow that openly submits all that left brain linear education: reading ,writing and math may possibly have some devastating mental side effects you call me so I can attempt to feel what you know as "hope." I am mindful you will not find one country on the planet that would suggest that so that suggests not one single country on the planet has cognitive ability any longer relative to elementary cause and effect relationships. Another way to look at it is, if a being does not have the cognitive ability to detect when they are harming the offspring which are the life spring of any species they are doomed to extinction. Another way to look at it is an adult only has one decision to make relative to the species and that is "Do you want to harm the offspring or make sure they are not harmed?" and the scribes always pick "Harm the offspring." The Male lion in that video killed a litter of cubs but our species mentally kills all the children and has for 5000 years. The scribes kill the children wholesale and then label their self "Civilization" as if to suggest they even know what civil is. This is the only reality the species needs to come to grips with: "What it comes down to is that modern society discriminates against the right hemisphere." - Roger Sperry (1973) Neurobiologist and Nobel Lauriat

Until we comes to grips with this reality as a spices [modern society discriminates against the right hemisphere] breathing does not matter, eating does not matter, drinking water does not matter.
Until as a species we understand this: [modern society discriminates against the right hemisphere] is relative to this:[reading, writing and arithmetic - the domain and strength of the left brain] peace does not matter, laws do not matter, money does not matter, governments do not matter, kindness does not matter, war does not matter, love does not matter, existence does not matter, because until we face the above reality we are nothing

but an abomination self harmer species as the result of our "wisdom" invention, education technology.

5/23/10 8:33 AM - Loss teaches the things luxury cannot. Loss either builds character or reveals it. Sincerity is a risk fool's delight in. Sincerity tends to be risky and deception tends to be a profession. A mistake is to learning as perfection is to stagnation.

[5. And all shall be smitten with fear
And the Watchers shall quake,
And great fear and trembling shall seize them unto the ends of the earth.]
Book of Enoch Chpater 1

"The pseudepigraphic Book of Enoch 31:4, dating from the last few centuries before Christ and purporting to be by the antediluvian prophet Enoch, describes the tree of knowledge: "It was like a species of the Tamarind tree, bearing fruit which resembled grapes extremely fine; and its fragrance extended to a considerable distance. I exclaimed, How beautiful is this tree, and how delightful is its appearance!" - WIKIPEDIA. COM

Let's contrast the spirit of how Genesis describes the tree of knowledge with the above verse.

[Genesis 3:6 And when the woman saw that the tree was good for food, and that it was pleasant to the eyes, and a tree to be desired to make one wise, she took of the fruit thereof, and did eat, and gave also unto her husband with her; and he did eat.]

[bearing fruit which resembled grapes extremely fine] = [it was pleasant to the eyes]

[and its fragrance extended to a considerable distance] = [was good for food(smelled good)]

[extremely fine] = [desired to make one wise]

All of these terms are interchangeable and essentially it is explaining the tree of knowledge is a perfect Trojan horse and thus irresistible. This is perhaps the key point explaining the tree of knowledge [a tree to be desired to make one wise.]
This comment [a tree to be desired to make one wise] is saying good intentions. One teaches the reading writing and math and their intentions are honorable relative to their perception but when taught to a small child it obliterates the chances that child can ever achieve the mental "third mind" or Holy Spirit aspect and so it is essentially a death sentence. There are so many cliché's to explain the reading, writing and math, "See no evil" = [it was pleasant to the eyes]. Speak and hear no evil = [desired to make one wise]. I read the scribes opinions on what exactly the tree of knowledge is and some say it is a grape, an apple, a fig, wheat, and one might suggest they are unable to see what is right in front of their nose. The moment a being understands the tree of knowledge is reading writing and math and after one gets the chance of them fully undoing

207

the mental damage caused by that "tree" are very slim indeed the world becomes very dark and because the scribes have such a prolonged emotional capacity in that state of mind caused by the education they perhaps cannot bear such reality or truth. The remedy is simply mental detachment for one second to the extreme but the scribes have trouble in distinguishing between that and literal detachment. Many years before the suggestion of the tree of knowledge in the Torah was a cylinder seal in Sumeria and it was a tree being guarded by a serpent. That's a pattern and the Sumerian are thought be the cradle of civilization relative to scribes civilization and they also developed written language first relative to the west about 5400 years ago and this all started in a historical place called Sumer, simply put these Sumerians invented writing and they had seals that depicted a serpent guarding the a tree and this was perhaps long before the struggle in Egypt between the scribes and the tribes. So writing itself because it is all linear based and thus sequential based and that is a left hemisphere aspect, civilization determines ones intelligence based on their writing skill among other things so it is a perfect drug and often fatal mentally and thus physically.

There is a show on TV about a man in South America and he was uneducated and he had a rented room that he stayed in with the wife and child and he had to go out every day to gather some sort of wood so he could make money to afford to pay the bank for the rent on this little house he lived in and he said "I must teach myself to read and write so I can get a better paying job." This story is the slavery. One is born into a world where this scribe "civilization" has control and one is in servitude to them because they have taken over everything. This is what this perception altering invention has done to the species. Simply put we can no longer make cognitive decisions or reasonable decisions so we just harm each other. In any control structure one is rewarded for submitting to being controlled and one is punished for resisting being controlled. The control structure makes all the rules. Why? Because it has all the weapons? Why? Because it can only control people using fear tactics. "You get education or you have poverty." is a fear tactic. Again it is not the education is the problem on its own merits it is the damage it mentally does to one and what one has to do to undo that damage is the problem. There are no studies on the physical effects all that education has on a person because there are no studies or even suggestions the education does any mental harm at all to a being relative to "common knowledge" and that is not a symptom the scribes have asked that question that is a symptom the control structure is unable to reason. It is probable that vast majority of physical illnesses are caused by being in the extreme left brain state caused by the education. Any stress or anxiety related illness is almost certainly caused by the education conditioning. The scribes are not even asking questions relative to if it is possible the education can harm the mind because they do not have the mental capacity to deal with a problem on that scale. The scribes are not even at the cognitive ability level to determine if it is reasonable to drill an oil rig in the middle of a gulf whose currents go all over the world. The scribes will argue "We need oil to breath" and that is their definition of mental complexity in their decision making processes. The scribes will create the problems and then pat their self on the back for attempting to solve the problem they create because they have no foresight to make determinations to avoid the problem to begin with.

Perhaps every nightmare one can think of goes back to those Sumerian seals with the image of a tree being guarded by a serpent. Perhaps the best way to fight the scribes is to allow them to keep making decisions because they are not capable of making any rational decisions so they hang their self by their very nature but the problem with that approach is they kill all the children in the process with their wisdom education. So this assumption of the supernatural aspect watching over everything or karma is at play does not really pan out because the situation is total darkness. Proper deeds being rewarded and improper deeds being punished is not happening perhaps at all. This is the truth:

[Mark 15:34 And at the ninth hour Jesus cried with a loud voice, saying, Eloi, Eloi, lama sabachthani? which is, being interpreted, My God, my God, why hast thou forsaken me?]

The cavalry is not coming to save you after you apply the remedy so you are you are going to have to rely on your mind and if you apply the remedy the full measure you are going to have a very good mind.
This is the truth:
The blind have lots of blind hope and the ones with sight understand that.

5/24/10 9:30 AM - Hallucinogen Persisting Perception Disorder: "Formerly classified as Post Hallucinogen Perception Disorder, Hallucinogen Persisting Perception Disorder involves re-experiencing the symptoms of hallucinogen without actual taking any of these substances.

What is a hallucinogen? Hallucinogens are drugs that cause distortions in a user's perceptions of reality. Users often see images, hear sounds, and feel sensations that seem real but do not exist. Some hallucinogens produce rapid, intense mood swings. The most common hallucinogens are LSD, PMA, 2 C-B, peyote, and certain varieties of mushrooms. The essential feature of Hallucinogen Persisting Perception Disorder (Flashbacks) is the transient recurrence of disturbances in perception that are reminiscent of those experienced during one or more earlier Hallucinogen Intoxications. The disturbance therefore causes marked distress. Complications of this disorder include suicidal behavior, Major Depression, and Panic Disorder."

This is what the education causes, Persisting Perception Disorder the only complication is the drug is all the left brain favoring education one gets as a child and that is the drug but outside of that this is a dead on description of the disorder.

[re-experiencing the symptoms of hallucinogen without actual taking any of these substances.]

Sense of time, strong and prolonged emotional capacity, strong sense of hunger, strong sense of fatigue, inability to concentrate. One that cannot concentrate cannot concentrate enough to determine they cannot concentrate. In this perception disorder one can no longer rely on their own perception they must rely on the perception of someone who has escaped the perception disorder.

[2 Timothy 4:1 ...., who shall judge the quick and the dead at his appearing and his kingdom;]

Only ones no longer experiencing the perception disorder (the quick) can judge who is in the perception disorder(the dead). It is logical a person with a perception disorder is in no condition to determine they have a perception disorder. Just because everyone you know perhaps has a strong sense of time does not mean strong sense of time is not a perception disorder. Just because nearly everyone you know has a nervous breakdown when they hear certain words, hear certain music or look at certain pictures does not mean they do not have a perception disorder. The comment when everyone around you is losing their head and you remain calm is saying, billions of people hallucinating does not mean it is not hallucinations. It is not important how many people have a strong sense of time or anxiety problems or strong sense of hunger it is still hallucinating.

[The most common hallucinogens are LSD, PMA, 2 C-B, peyote, and certain varieties of mushrooms.] This is wrong, the most common hallucinogens are years of left brain favoring reading, writing and math taught to small children and effects lasts for essentially permanently unless the remedy is applied. It will take you over a year to adjust to not hallucinating after you apply the remedy and at first you will assume you have started to hallucinate because the harsh reality is since you were a small child and started that education you have been hallucinating. You certainly knew your ABC's and how to count longer before you were six or seven and that is when the hallucinations started. I wouldn't go around telling people you never did any hallucinogens because you factually have been on the most powerful one there is for a vast portion of your life. When you apply the remedy and it takes effect you will assume you went insane and so you have to be mindful it is going to take about a year or more to adjust and that is an indication of how powerful that drug you are on is.

The remedy is not about creating damage it is about undoing damage or negating the hallucinogenic called the tree of knowledge.

[Hallucinogens are drugs that cause distortions in a user's perceptions of reality.] You perceive or observe time and that is abnormal and so you are hallucinating which simply means you have distortions in your perceptions of reality. You become physically weak when you do not eat for twenty-four hours or less and that is a distortion in your perception of reality. Your emotional capacity is so prolonged you can remain angry for well over a twenty four hour period and you can even remain in this state you call "in love" with things or people for well over a twenty four hour period and that is also abnormal and a symptom of distortion in perception of reality. I will rephrase that last part since you are hallucinating. The prolonged and profound emotional attachment to things and people is abnormal. A loss is a terrible thing to mind.

[Users often see images, hear sounds, and feel sensations that seem real but do not exist.]

After all that left brain favoring education one feels sensations that do not exist. You may hear a cuss word and your body has a panic attack. You may hear certain music and your body has a panic attack and you may say "Turn off that music I hate that song." You may say "Stop cussing you will go to hell and it is evil and it is bad." You may see a picture of a naked person or a dead person and say "I cannot look at that it is evil or bad." The picture, the music and the words and sounds are not evil you simply have distortions in your perceptions of reality. You have your favorite color and you have the colors you dislike and none of that exists you are just out of touch with reality. You do not have a favorite color it is just your perception is absolutely distorted. The reason you pass laws against the mild hallucinogen's like mushrooms and LSD is because you know how bad they can be because you know how bad the one you are on is, subconsciously. Another way to look at it is subconsciously you do not want anyone to take the mild hallucinogen's you only want people to take the infinitely powerful hallucinogenic you are on. People on LSD have altered perceptions for at most

214

twenty four hours and the one you are on induced by the education has lasted you since perhaps you were nine or ten. That first time you really got angry and upset all day long and you were bitter when something set you off is when you can understand the hallucinogenic kicked in. You were eight nine or maybe ten when you got very upset about something and you remained upset all day and now you can go into a rage over things that do not exists at all. Someone you know can say to your face "You are a loser" and you will remain upset about that for not only an hour but perhaps for the rest of your life.

[The essential feature of Hallucinogen Persisting Perception Disorder (Flashbacks) is the transient recurrence of disturbances in perception that are reminiscent of those experienced during one or more earlier Hallucinogen Intoxications.]
You have flashbacks and in fact all you do is have flashbacks and it is very easy to understand. You just think about one situation in your life where you were embarrassed or humiliated or ashamed or picked on and you will relive that experience with the time stamps and the emotions attached and every time you recall that you are having a flashback. Someone insulted you and now you never talk to them because they gave you a bad trip and it turned into a flashback and now you dislike that person perhaps for the rest of your life. I can walk up to you and say "You are a loser." in front of your peers and you will either hit me or have a nervous breakdown and perhaps never be able to forget that happened and thus have flashbacks about

it for the rest of your life. You may hit me if I say that to you because you are an emotional nightmare. You have transient recurrence of disturbances in perception. You are irritable because your mind is unsound and so the slightest thing can set you off. If the dishes are not washed properly you may freak out. If there is one thing out of your perceived order or control you might freak out. You have all your little vain hobbies to keep you from freaking out. As long as everything goes your way you don't have a nervous breakdown. You tend to get lost in your hallucination world and anything that enters your hallucination world and appears to conflict with how you perceive things is deemed evil, bad, hateful or unjust to you. You might be driving your car and someone might flick you off and that will upset you for the rest of the day and maybe a week. You may be dating a girl and she will dump you and you may never forget or recover from that and that will do permanent damage to your thoughts and you will have flashbacks about that for the rest of your life. You still remember the date that dumped you and you still are harmed mentally when you recall that memory and so you rather not think about it or bring it up because the flashbacks kick your ass on a daily basis. You have to do other drugs to take the edge off of the flashbacks you have accumulated in your mind after a lifetime of hallucinations induced by the education.

This sums up your mental state at all times [The disturbance therefore causes marked distress. Complications of this disorder include suicidal behavior, Major Depression, and Panic Disorder.]

[Marked distress][suicidal behavior] [Major Depression][Panic Disorder]
You don't forget anything I say to you and it effects your mood and that is caused because of this: [Some hallucinogens produce rapid, intense mood swings.]

So relative to psychology nearly every single disorder that is not relative to actual physiological brain damage falls under the umbrella of this disorder: Hallucinogen Persisting Perception Disorder: and that disorder is caused by all the years of left brain favoring education and there is no medicine that can cure that disorder because it is a mental disorder so it must be cured by a mental element and that is where the remedy comes in. This all relates perhaps to what is a human being after getting all that left brain favoring education?

A person that has this third mind aspect working is skillful in all wisdom and so a person that does not is skillful in all foolishness. One has to let go of the conspiracy aspect relative to the left brain education because it is not a conspiracy. Usually the simplest explanation is the proper explanation. It is so complex to suggest supernatural entities are making us get this education that in turn eliminates the third mind aspect because said education favors left hemisphere and combined with the fact the mind is very delicate when that education starts it mentally harms the being. It is simple to grasp five thousand years ago beings that had this third mind aspect were at a mental level of intelligence needed to create the written language and math and in learning those inventions inadvertently hindered their own minds. That version is very simple and thus likely to be the proper explanation. Although the time scale relative to a being that senses time appears vast the time scale is not vast. In the scale of human beings five thousand years ago is relatively recent. That is suggesting human beings went far longer without the mental hindering or were around far longer with this third mind aspect active than human beings were around with third mind aspect turned off. So all the details like technology for example are not causes of the mental hindering. Reading, writing and math when they first were invented were high technology and even today they are the pinnacle of our technological mountain. We have not surpassed reading, writing and math in any way technologically because all technology is relative to reading, writing and math. So all technology is relative to these three core branches: reading, writing and math so from that perspective we put all of our eggs in the reading, writing and math inventions but they had an unwanted unforeseen side effect and so we are sunk. The remedy itself only means we are returned to the minds we should have , the third mind aspect, but everything else remains the same relative to all the things created as a result of the tree of knowledge inventions. The argument has never been about technology relating to reading, writing and math, the argument has always been, make sure after you get the reading writing and math you apply the remedy to undo the unwanted mental side effects that result from learning that technology so you keep the third mind aspect. It is a simple concept that sometimes with technology one has to be mindful of its unwanted side effects and thus do things to compensate for that so that concept is not unreasonable and not a surprise. Using high technology sometimes requires certain compensation aspects and that is perhaps not supernatural. Sometimes you will hear when they are launching the space shuttle something like "We had to do something to compensate for the extra weight." Technology suggests complexity and as the complexity increases the compensation aspects tend to increase and so one must seek this harmony between complexity and compensation. Going down this road of supernatural only suggests one thing, we forgot who we are. You do not have another chance and you are not going to a better place than this place here perhaps. You may perceive life is short in your sense of time state of mind but I assure you when you get that third mind aspect back after you apply the remedy you will perceive life is infinitely long. Get it out of your head this "rewards after you die" aspect because all that thinking does is make you lazy and complacent. You got the education technology and now you have to compensate for that by applying the remedy so avoid assuming supernatural is going to do that for you because it never has and it never will. You have to compensate for the unwanted mental side effects of the education technology. You are in a perception dimension that makes you tend to pass the buck so to speak. This "nobody's fault" aspect relative to the education technology troubles you. Some seek conspiracy because they cannot tolerate simplicity. Everything will make sense once you get the third mind aspect back and perhaps little will make sense until you do. If I say anything I say we are too intelligent and so we must be mindful of that because with our level of intelligence relative to the third mind aspect we can get ourselves into many inadvertent traps that are difficult to get out of. Once you apply the remedy you will understand what "Traps that are difficult to get out of." means.

X = education technology
Y = get hypothalamus to give you its strongest signal and then ignore it
Z = third mind aspect restored

X + Y = Z

One can spend their whole life attempting to achieve (Y) or they can get it over with in one second. Achieving consciousness tends to be mindfully painful yet rewarding. You will not be accomplishing anything in life that will ever surpass applying the remedy because applying that remedy is the only meaning in life because that is where we are at as a species. We as a species are still in the infancy stages of adapting and compensating relative to this education technology we invented five thousand years ago. We are struggling and thus suffering as a result of attempts to compensate for this education technology we invented five thousand years ago. Because as a species we are failing to compensate for the education technology properly we are getting deeper and deeper into a hole and so we are suffering greatly and so something has to give soon. This education technology is putting a burden on everyone and putting a burden on the environment and so that suffering is a symptom our species is not doing too well at compensating for the education technology. The remedy is too harsh in contrast to what the education technology offers us and so as a species we show symptoms of that. A being that is in the final stages of depression and pondering taking their life as a result of having their mind hindered does not care about reading, writing and math. A being that is taking lots of drugs so they can escape what they perceive is reality when it is in fact that abnormal perception caused by the education technology does not care about reading, writing and math. A being that cuts their face so they will perceive they look good does not care about reading, writing and math. A being that stops eating food so they will perceive they are not obese even when they are not obese does not care about the education technology. A being that does drugs in hopes it will give them some creativity so they can formulate an idea to get them out of their situation does not care about the education technology. Once a being factors in all the side effects caused by the education technology and contrasts that with what the actual remedy is to undo that damage they will understand as a species we were not and are not ready for the education technology. We are writing checks our minds cannot cash. One can put every invention created as a result of the education technology on one side of a scale and then on the other side put all the mental capability ruined and all the suffering caused by being mentally hindered and see scales do not balance. If one can consider that scale without thinking about money for one second they can determine education technology is risky. Sometimes a popular decision is an unwise decision. Where would we be if we all had normal minds which mean's the third mind active and which means we were all skillful in all wisdom. I know where we are at now but the question is where should we be? We should not be here. We should not be in this mental trap we are in now. We should not be in the place of suffering but that is where we are at now because our education technology was a bit more than we bargained for. One has to be void of emotions to look at our species and calmly understand "We invented education technology and it screwed us up bad." We unknowingly drank out of a well full of poison and on a species wide level and that means we are not really healthy human beings anymore we are a very sick animal that is doing things only a very sick animal would do. A person that is in the end stages of rabies does not act like a person that does not have rabies. One cannot take a person in the end stages of rabies and say that is how human beings act so one has to clarify and suggest that person has rabies so their actions are more of an indication of their rabies infestation than an indication of how a healthy human being acts. The poison is so deadly no being has ever made one single dent in five thousand years relative to treating the poison on a species wide level and that is an indication of how deadly this mental poison is on our species relative to the education technology. Many have certainly tried but that means less than nothing to the curse. One may never get past this comment in the ancient texts:

222

[Genesis 3:14 And the LORD God said unto the serpent, Because thou hast done this(got the education technology), thou art cursed above all cattle(mentally hindered), and above every beast of the field; upon thy belly shalt thou go, and dust shalt thou eat all the days of thy life:]

Because we played around with the education technology we are cursed above everything and we will remain cursed until we kill our self off perhaps and you are worried about me because I don't use commas properly. I am cursed because I am aware we are cursed so I am still cursed. We are cursed above all cattle because of our education technology and some being tells me "Try not to say the word "I" because the scribes might think you have an ego."

There is only one thing that matters when you are cursed and that is seeking the remedy to the curse but first one has to detect the curse and that just so happens to be a part of the curse, the inability to detect the curse. What that means is one has to pray to the universe that one being will break the curse and explain to them so they can understand the remedy to the curse because if that does not happen said being will not be breaking the curse. The curse is so strong we inadvertently created the aspect that enables the curse five thousand years ago and right now as a species we have no idea we did that and that indicates we are in some sort of trauma as a species. There was a video I watched about a guy who got hit by a train and it split open his back from waist to neck and he was sitting upright and blood was everywhere and a person told him to stay seated and help will be by shortly and the guy tried to stand up and he was asking for his glasses. As a species we are totally oblivious to this curse the education technology has given us. If there was hope one perhaps would think at least one country on the planet would have figured it out by now yet no country on the planet has even a slight clue. We have all these illusions of technology yet none of them on an absolute scale has a slightest ability to detect the curse created inadvertently five thousand years ago. What that suggests is we have a lot of little trinkets that are worthless. Does your electron microscope tell you the species is mentally hindered and keeps mentally hindering itself and does that microscope tell you the remedy to the curse because if it does not it is perhaps totally worthless. Does all the gold in the universe explain to you the remedy and the reason for the remedy to the curse because if it does not it is perhaps totally worthless. Go around your house and ask everything you own what the remedy to the curse is and why the remedy is needed and you can determine how much your possessions are worth rather swiftly. Ghandi was reported to say something along the lines of "I like their Christ but I don't care for the Christians." That was a nice way of saying , I like that guy who put his money where his mouth is and applied the remedy but I do not care for the ones who ride his coat tails and make billions of dollars off of his coat tails and don't talk about the remedy or apply the remedy." Talk does not mean anything to the curse and words do not mean anything to the curse and neither words or nor talk perhaps is going to get your hypothalamus to give you the death signal so you can ignore the signal.

The ego or pride as you know it is one of the main symptoms of the curse and the remedy forces one to kill that pride or ego. Another way to look at it is in a dark and spooky place when your mind says "Run or something spooky will kill you" the only reason a person would ever run is if they perceive they have value and value is relative to ego and pride. That single concept makes applying the remedy nearly impossible. Some scribes will attempt to use their linear pinprick logic to explain how that is not truth yet they will only confuse their self further. One scribe said the fruit on the tree of knowledge is wheat. One scribe said the fruit on the tree of knowledge is grapes. The point is the scribes are looking for physical when the curse is cerebral which means the curse is perception relative. There is no technology on this planet that can detect this curse yet this third mind aspect human beings achieve when their mind is in a unified state can detect the curse and also explain the remedy to the curse effortlessly. This suggests the technology of today may be attempts of human beings to attempt to emulate what we have lost. Our education technology cost us our third mind aspect. If the third mind aspect can detect the curse caused by the education technology and also determine the cure for the curse yet all other technology cannot do that, then all other technology is not even at the intelligence level of the third mind aspect. A computer can never achieve intuition that right brain and this third mind aspect achieves so before one goes on touting how intelligent machines will be one day they must first understand they will never come close to this third mind aspect intuition all human beings are born with. We have been mentally hindered so greatly by the education technology we actually perceive we can create something more intelligent than our naturally occurring third mind aspect. This telling the future aspect is what the intuition aspect is relative to but it is also relative to making informed decisions, so to speak. The third mind aspect is so powerful one can actually detect what their thought processes are. For example I can see a comment and the spirit of that comment is my first look intuition but then after that is done the pondering starts and within an hour or so relative to a clock all these patterns relative to that comment start forming concepts but this is not like I am thinking real hard, this is going on in the background as I do other things and when a solid understanding is achieve that understanding is thrown into this sea of concepts and it waits for another concept that may be a pattern so it can come to the surface again. So for example in an early volume I suggested this accident meant either I went to extreme left brain, extreme right brain or an unknown state of mind. So now I understand that unknown state of mind I mentioned perhaps near two years ago is this third mind state. So my intuition is nearly two years ahead of "me". A scribe will perhaps assume "Oh he changes his mind a lot." because a scribe is mentally dead in the water. A scribe has one "ah ha "sensation in a lifetime and that is it if they are lucky. This third mind is "ah ha" sensation but at first I was unaware what exactly happened but the first thing I thought on the day I got the "ah ha "sensation was "I lost my sense of time." The mind is just like a gun. A shotgun shoots its pellets in a wide area and that is the sense of time state of mind and the third mind state of mind is the now and that is like a regular bullet that is very compressed into one area. The no sense of time aspect is the key to considering everything is a decision making process. Nothing is too old and nothing is too new relative to concepts to consider relative to decision making. One scribe said I sounded new age and I fell out of my chair.

5/25/10 12:07 AM - Differential equations relative to economics are essentially based on time. All economic systems are doomed to failure because of supply and demand. Because there is perhaps never an infinite amount of supply, in time supply will be used up and what speeds that up is efficiency. As efficiency increases supply decreases although initially it appears supply increases with efficiency.

One can look at lobster fishing. As soon as deep sea ships were invented the lobster supply went up but now there is a shortage of lobster and so efficiency created the shortage. An economic system is relative to greed because money is more important than supply so an economic system seeks high efficiency and low supply because that equates to maximum profits but because profits are not infinite as profit efficiency increases supply of profits decreases. Because money is artificial and the supply product tends to not be artificial it means in the end the money will be all that will be left and it will be worthless. Money without a supply is worthless.

P = profits

E = efficiency
D = demand
S = supply
T = Time

So the basic concept of economics is:

T + E + S = P

This is just saying the faster and more economical you create the supply the more profits you make.

So this equation is the down side of economics:

T + E – D = P

This is just saying the faster or more economical you getting the supply the sooner the demand decreases. This creates a situation where it is logical one would harvest a supply as fast as possible before the demand decreases. So these two equations are a paradox.

(T + E + S = P) = (T + E – D = P) This means the more efficient you are at creating supply the more profits you will make and the less profits you will make. The time factor in economics is what ensures economies collapse. Because anything is allowed to make profits as fast as possible(time) the supply is secondary. This means one either has to find alternatives to the current supply or face the extinction of the supply. The problem with that is there tends not to be infinite supplies. So this means the economic system cannot last because it is based on whom ever gets there first and uses up the supplies gets the profits and the result of that is not a factor. If there is a supply of fish in a pond whomever gets to that pond first and can harvest all those fish and sell them is the one who makes profits and the fish are not important only the efficiency and time are relative because they are relative to profits. So the time factor in economics means the faster one can harvest a supply the better and that ensures economic collapse. A person can get a dip net to catch the fish in the pond or they can get a gill net and cover the whole pond and catch all the fish in one event and that is the most efficient and time saving method and thus it is the most economical method and thus it is the most profitable method so it is assumed relative to economics to be the proper method. In economics profits are more important than sensibility. In economics as efficiency decreases sensibility increases yet as sensibility increases profits decrease. Think about the oil rig leak. If sensibility was at play then the oil company would have had 100 pressure valve backups on the pipe to ensure there was no way the oil would leak but that would kill their profits. Because economics really is just profits nothing can ever trump profits or one goes bankrupt. This means economics is not relative to sensibility it is relative to profits so one has to choose between the two because one cannot have both. In an economic system one is in competition with others so one is mindful to be as efficient as possible but the more efficient they are the less money they make in the long run because the supply is increased or runs out or is increased and then runs out.

The invention of the internet appeared to be creating a new supply aspect so it was assumed to be this "cash cow" but in reality it created a surplus in information and the more information a person has the more efficient a person becomes and the more efficient a person becomes the sooner the profits dry up. The internet destroyed the economic system because people have become addicted to information and information is given freely on the internet. I highly doubt people go from door to door selling encyclopedias anymore. I highly doubt newspaper sales are increasing. The lower income human beings are finding information given freely is an alternative to material aspects and so they slowly stop thinking about material aspects and substitute that craving with craving information. The human species is slowly substituting material desires for key strokes and so the economy collapses because people substitute this supply and demand aspect for information and information is relative to the observer. Every day a person is on the internet is another day that person is not using up as many raw materials. For example before the internet a person felt they had to "go out" to experience life, like one might go out to eat, then watch a movie, then go shopping and all of this encouraged the economy but now a person can sit home and explore the world through in their home and get the same satisfaction without "contributing" to the economic system. The more a person thinks the less material aspects matter. A person may go on the internet and look up a location they want to visit and in their research they may reach a point in understanding that they realize they understand enough about the location they do not need to actually travel there. As creativity increases desire for materiel things decreases. The internet encourages creativity because a person becomes just a mind behind a keyboard. One goes to a search engine and they are faced with a blank topic entry form and whatever they type in they are certain a lifetime of information will pop up when they hit the search button unless of course they type in my name or their name. So the trend that will result is the control structure will find a way to charge by the minute for the internet to compensate for the fact every minute a person is online is a minute they are not contributing the economic system. The internet is not economic friendly because it is nearly an unlimited supply relative to information. The internet is a common man's dream and a control structures nightmare.

5/25/10 2:16 PM - Words remind us of our inability to fully communicate an experience through them. Time postpones inevitability. The enemy understands your faults better than you do. Wisdom is foolishness with experience. Wisdom is experienced foolishness. Knowledge is understanding how far ones ignorance goes. What one thinks is not always what one thought.

[Mark 8:34 And when he had called the people unto him with his disciples also, he said unto them, Whosoever will come after me, let him deny himself, and take up his cross, and follow me.]
[Luke 12:51 Suppose ye that I am come to give peace on earth? I tell you, Nay; but rather division:]

[let him deny himself] = [division:]

Both parties relative to the sense of time perception dimension and the no sense of time perception dimension must deny their self at all times and that requires discipline. A being in the sense of time perception dimension wants to feed their ego and pride so they must avoid doing that and a being in the no sense of time perception dimension wants to feed their holistic perception and they must avoid doing that.

X = sense of time perception dimensions
Y = no sense of time perception dimension

X sees parts and that a left brain trait so in order for them to deny their self they have to see holistically. A simple example would be if one dislikes certain music they listen to it until they are indifferent and that is denying their perception.

Y sees holistically because in the third mind state right hemisphere traits rule so one tends to see everything as good so one is horrible judge relative to their perception so they would seek division to deny their perception.

So then we have beings that apply this remedy and have (Y) perception running around saying "Everything is fantastic and nothing is wrong and love, love, love." and because they do not deny their self or their perception, they are caught up in their own perception. So Luke 12:51 is Jesus saying "I applied the remedy and I see everything is perfect or I see holistically so I seek division."

[Luke 12:51 Suppose ye that I am come to give peace on earth? I tell you, Nay; but rather division:]
One can think about stories about a wise man going off and isolating their self from the world and living alone. The wise beings in the ancient texts resisted that because they denied their self which means their perception after they applied the remedy. Although one may have observed them as self righteous because they were saying "Your scribes are viper and demons and Satan." that was really their efforts to deny their perception which was saying "Everything is good and perfect and nothing is wrong." It is simple to find division in the sense of time perception dimension because one perceives many parts but it requires discipline to see division in the no sense of time holistic perception dimension. Certainly there are many who applied this remedy and said "I feel much better now and I see everything is good. Thank you and good night."

So this comment [let him deny himself] applies to both sides. What that means is one never reaches the top of the mountain so to speak and that creates this infinite progression aspect. One cannot compare a person in the sense of time perception dimension to a person in the no sense of time perception dimension because the two dimensions are opposite.
The ones that see parts have to deny that parts aspect and try to see holistically and that is achieved by applying the remedy the full measure and the ones that see holistically must deny that holistic aspect and try to see parts but they cannot apply a remedy to see parts so they have to always keep this deny yourself aspect

in mind or they will just give up. The trend is not for ones that see holistically to go out and speak about the dangers of the education technology the trend is to see the education technology as "good" and never say anything about it. I could just write a book and say "Everything is fantastic and change nothing and everything is sugar and milk" and you may write me letters and tell me I am great, that's easy street. The battle is not easy street. "Lets all just get along.", that's easy street. As a species and because of our education technology invention we are infinitely far away from "Lets all just get along." There is no coming to consciousness on a species level without extreme pain and that is extreme treason and treason is the ninth circle of hell. There is nowhere to run no matter which side you are on, the only difference is one side understands that and the other side is ignorant about that. After you apply the remedy you have two choices: You can get caught up in the holistic perception or you can go back into hell and attempt to suggest the remedy to others. The former choice is a symptom of ego and the latter choice is a symptom of selflessness. It's a simple concept that a person runs out of a burning house and they are safe but they are aware there are still people in that burning house and to add a little challenge the people in the burning house are blind to the fact the house is burning so they will tend to not want to leave the burning house. So with that mind one is not really saving people one is denying their self further, one is prostrating their self further, one is tormenting their self further by going back into the burning house they have escaped to try to communicate to people who do not even see the house is burning. There is an aspect that once one applies the remedy they are better than the ones who have not but in reality once one applies the remedy they are just willing to take more punishment than the ones who have not applied the remedy. I am not better than anyone I am just pleased with the hottest coals. I would stop breathing if the coals were anything less than infinitely hot. The hottest coals make the strongest steel. The log in the eye is the perception. Mistakes are the key to wisdom so seek mistakes. If one tries to say the perfect thing they will never say anything. Every person gets to hear the remedy because no person is intelligent enough to know how every person will react to it. Some see clearly when they hear the remedy and some fight harshly when they hear the remedy. One is not trying to make people apply the remedy one is trying to better their own ability to explain the remedy and so the ideal situation is a place where everyone mocks the remedy because that is where the greatest progression potential exists and that is perhaps why many diciples got butchered and many other beings who attempted this remedy suggestion. Everything has to be considered in the reverse. In the world of the scribes the concept is "Don't bring unwanted harm to yourself" so in the no sense of time perception dimension the reality is "Seek the hottest coals." You will only get better after you apply the remedy by sticking your head out of the rabbit hole. The thorns on a rose keeps one honest. Tyrants tend to assume their subjects are the problem.

This is a comment by Roger Sperry "What is needed to break the vicious spiral is a world-wide change in attitudes, values, and social policy. As Einstein put it, "We need a substantially new manner of thinking if mankind is to survive.""

"There appears to be two modes of thinking, verbal and non-verbal, represented rather separately in left and right brain hemispheres respectively, and that our educational system, as well as science in general, tends to neglect the non-verbal form of intellect." Roger continued, "What it comes down to is that modern society discriminates against the right hemisphere of the brain."- Roger Sperry

So we have the education technology that favors left hemisphere and because it is taught at an age long before the frontal lobe even developers it hinders mental development and that means how one thinks is affected. How one thinks is relative to what one perceives and the education technology alters what one perceives which means it makes one a schizophrenic which is simply a person that's perception is out of alignment with reality.

"What is needed to break the vicious spiral is a world-wide change in attitudes, values, and social policy. "
[What is needed to break the vicious spiral]
[vicious spiral] = [the 3 R's: reading, writing and arithmetic -- the domain and strength of the left brain]
[world-wide] = [mankind] = [modern society] = the scribes.

[attitudes,] = The scribes perceive reading writing and math is desired to make one wise so that attitude needs to be adjusted to , reading writing and math has unintended mental consequences when taught to small children and so the children must be warned of that prior to getting the education and given a choice of education methods, strictly oral education until they are older, and not discriminated against if they select oral education, and the children that elect reading, writing and math must be taught the remedy to the unintended mental side effects of the traditional education.

[Values] = The scribes perceive anyone who does not get their brand of education is stupid or dumb and thus discriminates against them. This is evident in a simple equation.

X = amount of written education
Y = pay scale
Z = respect or profile in society

$$X + Z = Y$$

Simply put if you have a DR. in front of your name you get paid well and if you have no title in front of your name you are digging ditches and that title in front of your name is relative to the amount of written education you received.

[social policy] = compulsory attendance law = A child must start the written education by the age of six or seven and even if they are taught at home they must be taught reading, writing, and math by law.

So this comment by Einstein ["We need a substantially new manner of thinking if mankind is to survive.""] is saying, The traditional education is destroying our minds and thus altering how we think and no creature is viable with a hindered mind and if that is not addressed above everything else we will kill ourselves off. These beings Einstein and Sperry attempted to explain the situation with a sort of civility or calm manor. If one got the education one is factually schizophrenic and thus out of touch with reality and is harming children by making them get the same education conditioning that was forced on them and they are not even aware of it. Thus one must attempt to apply the remedy and until one does they are not mentally viable as a being.

[if mankind is to survive.] We have to go through the ninth circle of hell, treason and it may kill us all but if we do not do that we will all die off. Einstein had some regrets about assisting the scribes to make nukes because he slowly understood he handed nukes to lunatics. If you sense time mindfully you are schizophrenic as a result of the education technology and thus you are a threat to yourself and those around you. Why don't you go tell the scribes how much you love them for what they did to your infinitely powerful mind with their wisdom education.

This is an important concept to understand although Sperry was quite timid in his explanation.

"There appears to be two modes of thinking, verbal and non-verbal, represented rather separately in left and right brain hemispheres respectively, and that our educational system, as well as science in general, tends to neglect the non-verbal form of intellect."

Written education favors left hemisphere and that is essentially what modern society is based on, reading and math, verbal communication. Right hemisphere deals with no-verbal communication and that is relative to right brain intuition which you might know as telepathy. So the scribes kill the telepathy, non verbal communication to favor the verbal communication. There is a concept about the aliens communicate using telepathy, that's us but the scribes hinder or turn that aspect off not because they are mean it is because they are insane and know not what they do. So right brain intuition is the telepathy aspect of our communication ability and the traditional education turns it off and that is what this comment means [our educational system, as well as science in general, tends to neglect the non-verbal form of intellect."]= we are materialistically heavy and cerebrally light. So the third mind aspect which is the mind that one has after they apply the remedy can use verbal and non-verbal communication. A scribe can only use verbal communication because their right hemisphere intuition is hindered by the education. Again this is not a conspiracy because the ruler scribes mentally hinder their own children and are not even aware of it. The ruler scribes are going along with the herd just like the common scribes are. Going along with the herd means everyone is convinced reading, writing, and math has absolutely no unwanted or unintentional mental side effects and that is because the education veils their right brain ambiguity so the scribes cannot question their self or their deeds. The concept focus on the log in your eye is in part suggesting to society, "Look at yourself, question what you are doing, ask questions about the education, why do you take everyone's word that education is flawless? Forget about your emotions, ego and pride for a second and be an honest observer."

5/26/10 5:45 PM - This comment is explaining why Jesus was killed and who he was killed by.
[Luke 5:21 And the scribes and the Pharisees began to reason, saying, Who is this which speaketh blasphemies? Who can forgive sins, but God alone?]

[scribes and the Pharisees] = any human being that was exposed to reading, writing, and math, and even a person cannot read or write but they have some math skills in order to use money. Money is relative to math and this is relative to the comment money is the root of all evil, and modern society is the root of evil because it is based on money and thus math so it is a given a person will get the mental hindering because they learn math in order to use the monetary system in modern society. So Jesus was telling the truth that he could cure people of this curse, the mental hindering caused by the tree of knowledge with his "deny yourself" and "those who lose their life (mindfully) preserve it" and thus they would escape these prolonged thoughts like greed, envy, gluttony (sin) simply because they would return the right brain random access thoughts and be unable to maintain those "sin" thoughts, but the catch is Jesus is explaining this to crazy, insane, cursed beings. Another way to look at it is Jesus is talking to beings that got the tree of knowledge and they do not have the cognitive ability to understand what he was saying so they assume he was saying "I am God" and considering the scribes are insane Jesus had a cognitive ability that in contrast to the scribes was God like. It all comes back to the same point, if you doubt the remedy works attempt to apply it and until you apply it keep your mouth shut because you factually do not have cognitive ability to make judgments and the proof of that is you do not believe all that left brain favoring education harms children because you keep mentally harming them generation after generation. A serial killer at least understands he is killing people but the scribes are not at that level of cognitive ability. Jesus was attempting to explain the remedy to the mental hindering caused by the tree of knowledge and the scribes got the tree of knowledge and their cognition was nil and so they misunderstood him and killed him and just before he died Jesus made this comment.

[Mark 15:34 And at the ninth hour Jesus cried with a loud voice, saying, Eloi, Eloi, lama sabachthani? which is, being interpreted, My God, my God, why hast thou forsaken me?]

[My God, my God, why hast thou forsaken me?] = The situation relative to this "curse" is so bad when beings that apply the remedy fully attempt to communicate with the scribes they can be misunderstood to the degree they are killed by the scribes. In spirit the above comment is saying "All I did was tell them a common obvious problem I detected and the remedy to that problem and the scribes nailed me to a cross and let me die in the sun." So this means even at the time of Jesus the scribes could not handle being told the education technology had flaws and had a strong aversion to anyone that suggested it did. It is one thing to be just [skillful in all wisdom] and it is another thing to also be eager to the tell the truth about the education technology and be [skillful in all wisdom] and perhaps timidity is relative to that.

X = "tribes" that never have been exposed at all to a math system or a writing system and have had no contact with beings that have been exposed to the education technology.

Y = Beings that have been exposed

Z = Third mind Holy Spirit aspect (no sense of time perception dimension)

A = Exposed state of mind.(sense of time perception dimension)

B = abnormal

C = normal

X + Z = C

$$Y + A = B$$

So this means we are under the influence of the third mind or holy spirit aspect where we are [skillful in all knowledge] if we are not exposed to the education technology at all. So if one thinks about the garden of Eden concept, we literally ate off the tree of knowledge and fell from grace (veiled right hemisphere and eliminated the chance the third mind aspect or holy spirit can happen unless one applies the remedy.] So that fall from grace was a symptom in part of how subtle and devastating the mental damage is. Slowly over a short period of time perhaps less than 500 years after the invention of Sumerian language and math we became so mentally hindered we could not even tell we became mentally hindered by the education technology. There is a person that is drunk but can still communicate and then there is the level of a person drunk that is completely out of touch with reality and maybe even unconscious. So we as a species as a result of this education technology are literally in an altered state of consciousness called unconsciousness in contrast to how we are in the third mind state or the no sense of time perception dimension. So these tribes that have not been exposed are the "Holy Spirit" at full strength and sop it is logical they would be very different that the scribes who have been exposed. If one just thinks off the top of their head how these tribes are treated and look at as being "less" that the world of the scribes that is in line with the comment that modern society discriminates against right hemisphere. The tribes that have had no exposure at all to the scribes ways should be disseminated against the most because they are the purest form of the holy spirit relative to the fact they are exhibiting human being deeds and actions consistent with living in harmony and not be greedy, lustful, envious or wrathful in contrast to the scribes. So when society says "You want us to go back to the stone age?" they are really saying "We are pleased with the altered and abnormal state of mind dimension." The scribes perhaps are not at the level to understand we are docile mammals. We do not kill each other and destroy the environment for some scribe inventions called paper money. We tend to live in harmony and are quite docile and very cerebral. We made this education technology with our great cerebral capacity and it annihilated our minds and our cerebral capacity and that is what "is" and that is why the remedy "is" and that is reality relative to the current state of our species.

It is risky explaining to the scribes their golden calf the education technology harms children.

Roger Sperry - "What is needed to break the vicious spiral is a world-wide change in attitudes, values, and social policy."

Einstein -, "We need a substantially new manner of thinking if mankind is to survive.""

[Genesis 2:17 But of the tree of the knowledge of good and evil, thou shalt not eat of it: for in the day that thou eatest thereof thou shalt surely die.]

[social policy.] = [manner of thinking] = [tree of the knowledge of good and evil]

[vicious spiral] = [if mankind is to survive.] =[for in the day that thou eatest thereof thou shalt surely die.]

The combination of the three comments is :

We need to break the vicious spiral which is relative to our social policy relative to the tree of knowledge of good and evil which is relative the left brain favoring reading, writing, and math or mankind will surly die. You may have a positive attitude relative to this situation but I assure you that is your blindness talking. As a species we have adopted this mentally hindered perception state into our existence. Another way to look at it is our species has attempted to survive with one hemisphere and the less of the two hemispheres to boot. We cannot survive with just one hemisphere and it shows. A judge once told me "If you want to kill yourself no one can stop you." and that is exactly the truth relative to our species relative to this left brain favoring education technology. Our species is killing itself with this education technology and no one is going to stop us from doing that. Your laws, governments, countries mean nothing because as a species we are killing ourselves off with the education technology and we as a species collective are not even aware of it. After you apply this remedy, before you think about censoring your testimony, relative to how powerful your mind is once it is restored, you be mindful we are already dead as a species.

It is not probable we will wake up and question our education technology and look into addressing its unwanted mental side effects so it is probable we are dead as a species. You hear what would happen if crazy people got a hold of the nukes, well the crazy people are modern society, the scribes.

Modern society is the ones that discriminate against right hemisphere via their education technology and they are not even aware of it at all, and only crazy people know not what they do.

[Roger continued, "What it comes down to is that modern society discriminates against the right hemisphere of the brain."]

Eat, drink and be merry for tomorrow we die. That comment is our species mantra. That comment should be every countries motto. The adults tell the little children, "let me teach you the monetary system." and they are really teaching them math. All the children are running around counting their money, their pennies and are unaware they are conditioning right hemisphere into a subconscious state. The little children are doing that because the adults are doing that. The little children are emulating the adults and the adults are lunatics. The adults were children and they emulated the adults. This comment : "What it comes down to is that modern society discriminates against the right hemisphere of the brain." is saying, if there is a devil modern society is the devil and it is called the scribes who love their golden calf education technology and they push it on all the children with reckless abandon and then brag how wise they are for doing so. The situation we are in a species is like a cancer patient in stage five determining they want to live after all. So any ideals you have about what matters the most in life that does not have addressing the education technology situation in the forefront is strictly delusional thinking. That is a nice way of saying everything you can think of in life does not matter at all in contrast to addressing the education technology now. Whatever you have to say is fine by me. Whatever you say to the scribes in attempting to communicate to them about the education technology situation is fine by me. Be creative, you are dealing with insane beings, the scribes that harm children by the millions and do not even believe they do. One of the very first things you be mindful of after you apply the remedy is how vast the numbers of the scribes are. When you are falling from a cliff do the words you say cushion your landing? I keep assuming what I say is common knowledge.

One way to look at it is the education technology mentally harmed you and you are mentally dying and so you are going to have to fight with everything you have to restore your mind and it is going to be painful mentally. You are factually not going to read this book and understand the remedy and rush off to apply it because you perhaps are not suffering enough. I assure you the ninth circle of hell , treason, is very dark but you will not apply the remedy the full measure until you are in that circle. After the education one is essentially mentally dead in contrast to how a person is after they apply the remedy so one has to fight that mental death because it is easy to remain mentally dead and it is nearly impossible to defeat that mental death and the symptom one is starting to fight to wake up is depression, anger and spite of everything. One way to look at it is one has to go to the extreme of crazy to reach consciousness and that is just the remedy to the mental conditioning caused by learning the education technology at such a young age. The anger and depression is equal to how intelligent you are. To explain that one can look at it like a human being is infinitely intelligent but the education turns one down to about ten percent of that intelligence and so one has to go through this depression aspect to get back their mind. You may perceive you do not want to go through the angry and depressed part but it has to do with mindset in order to apply the remedy. It is like having a cast on your arm and just before the cast comes off it gets very itchy. It is best to just go out and apply the remedy but even at that you are going to go through this river of anger. You will not seek the shadow of death and when it arrives, fear not, if you are happy even slightly. Try to keep everything on the mental level which means no matter how depressed you get that is simply the itchy part and a good sign that you are mentally starting to be aware. Do not listen to the scribes once you become depressed and start considering the remedy because they are factually insane and have no idea what they are talking about. The scribes would not have mentally killed you to begin with if they knew what they were doing so do not rely on them to advise you. In your left brain state of mind you want advice and you want to give up easily and you want the easy way out. You have to start getting away from your herd mentality. The herd is running off a cliff so stay away from the herd. You are better off alone mentally than surrounded by a herd of blind men. This means when you are around the scribes you look at everything they say to you as a test. The scribes will mock you and attempt to break your will in every way imaginable and you remind yourself you can think on your own. You remind yourself the scribes put you in this situation and now you have to apply this remedy so consider the scribes illusions of stupidity. Look at the scribes like dirt and so when they speak you dust their words off. There will perhaps not be one single scribe on this planet that will suggest applying this remedy is wise. There is perhaps not one single scribe on this planet that perceives seeking the shadow of death and then submitting mindfully when it arrives is wise. There is perhaps not one single scribe on this planet that will suggest losing your life mindfully to preserve your life mindfully is wise. If you are even pondering applying the remedy it is a miracle so do not let the scribes bend you away from your pondering of the remedy. Be mindful the vast majority of beings that get this education technology are fatalities and will never ever restore their mind, ever. What that means is misery loves company and there are lots of miserable beings that are infinitely wise but have been turned down to ten percent mental capacity and they do not want anyone else subconsciously to restore their mind. The scribes do not want anyone to wake up because they are subconsciously aware they will never wake up. Once you apply the remedy it is warming up time so the only aspect that is important is applying the remedy and getting into the proper frame of mind to apply the remedy. There is a concept that says it gets dark before the light. Dark is the ninth circle of hell, treason and one has to go through there to get to light. There are no exceptions so avoid looking for a short cut. You seek a short cut because the remedy is daunting relative to your perception. The scribes have made you very timid with their education technology. The remedy is simple on an absolute scale. The remedy in concept is simply getting into a situation your hypothalamus gives you the strongest fight or flight signal it can and then you ignore that signal and that is the remedy in its entirety. Simple that is.

Looking at the comment below the word fear pops up many times.

[1 John 4:18 There is no fear in love; but perfect love casteth out fear: because fear hath torment. He that feareth is not made perfect in love.]

One can replace the word fear with timidity.
[He that is timid is not made perfect in love.]
[There is no timidity in love]
[but perfect love casteth out timidity]
[because timidity hath torment.]

If you get timid when you hear certain words or hear certain music or look at certain pictures that is a symptom. This comment is simply saying the scribes in learning their education technology become very timid because the education affects the hypothalamus and so they are tormented. The scribes are tormented because their mind is unsound and that is the cause of the torment and one aspect of that is timidity. The deeper reality is a scribe cannot tell they are being tormented in general but the depressed and suicidal scribe's are near the treason stage or in it. Another way to look at it is a scribe does not know what a sound mind is like because their mental development was aborted by the education technology starting at the age of six or seven or earlier. So a scribe will proclaim they are not tormented because all they know is torment. Once one applies the remedy they understand what torment was, and what blindness was and what being lost was, but perhaps not until. The mindset of a depressed person is "There is no hope." and they are right on the money relative to their observations but they perceive it is just them. The depressed perceive the problem is them so they are focused on the log in their eye. The scribes will tell you the suicidal are looking for attention and that just shows their lack of foresight, cognition, comprehension and compassion and those are all symptoms the scribes lack intuition, a right brain trait. The scribes actually mock human beings they mentally destroyed with the education technology unknowingly, that are attempting to wake their self up unknowingly, which are the depressed. The scribes tend to create problems and then they cannot fix them and so they assume the problem is to complex because the scribes cannot imagine it is because they are mentally hindered because right hemisphere deals with complexity. The scribes give pills to people who they mentally hindered with the education and the scribes make lots of money off of that but they never cure anyone of the mental hindering, they at best just keep that person from waking up. If the scribes were out to help anyone they would not hinder people to begin with using the education and even after that if they were out to help anyone they would tell them the remedy but there is no money to make in telling people the remedy because the remedy is a one person show and one time permanent fix and so there is no long term money to make off the remedy.

This is truth -
"In humans, the frontal lobe reaches full maturity around only after the 20s, marking the cognitive maturity associated with adulthood"
" If you reflect back upon our own educational training, we have been traditionally taught to master the 3 R's: reading, writing and arithmetic -- the domain and strength of the left brain"

Roger Sperry said quite simply in 1973 "What it comes down to is that modern society discriminates against the right hemisphere of the brain." He won a Nobel prize in neurobiology

How does modern society mentally hinder people unknowingly by discriminating against right hemisphere? reading, writing and arithmetic -- the domain and strength of the left brain"

The only remedy to this, because said education makes the hypothalamus very hyperactive is to condition oneself away from fear or timidity. The full measure version of this as Jesus suggested is "Those who lose their life (mindfully) preserve it" = "Seek the shadow of death and then fear not"(Psalms 23:4)

In Buddhism the remedy is simply to go to a spooky place alone at night like a cemetery and see if you can get the hypothalamus to give you the strongest fight or flight signal it can, the death signal and then meditate which means ignore that signal. The amygdala will remember that and soon the right hemisphere traits will be restored. One will know it has worked fully when they lose their sense of time, so if one has a sense of time, that proves the education mentally hindered them by veiling the right brain paradox from their perception.

So one seeks the "shadow" of death and (deny's their self)(Jesus' suggestion) Luke 9:23

Seek the shadow of death and fears not (Abraham first suggested fear not) Genisis 15:1

Or one seeks the shadow of death and then when it arrives one submits - submission is suggested by Mohamed and is the core doctrine of Islam.
This shows religion is simply methods to undo the mental damage caused by the tree of knowledge, reading writing and math and perhaps nothing more. I don't expect a scribe to agree with that because they are mentally hindered but Jesus was compared to the scribes, the ones who got the education and did not apply the remedy.

[Mark 1:22 And they were astonished at his doctrine: for he taught them as one that had authority, and not as the scribes.]
Scribes are the ones that sense time.

All of these methods are effective as a remedy to the tree of knowledge. Tree of knowledge being reading, writing and arithmetic -- the domain and strength of the left brain"

[That was one of my vanity emails to someone]

Now before one goes running their mouth about truth and wisdom and justice and compassion one first must at least reach a level of cognitive ability to understand the education is factually hindering children simply because the child's frontal lobe does not develop until the child is in their 20's so the education effectively aborts the child's cognitive ability because it veils the child's right brain intuition and thus effects their perception and perception is relative to cognitive ability.

5/28/10 12:34 AM - Grief is relative to wisdom because understanding is relative to awareness and awareness is relative to foresight of eventualities. Awareness of a trap is one level of grief but understanding one cannot escape the trap is another level. A lesson learned from mental action is intelligence. Nothing anticipates something and grief anticipates nothing. Nothing is ready for anything yet grief only seeks change. When you don't recall what you wrote, you are writing well.

5/29/10 1:48 AM -

[Daniel 2:1 And in the second year of the reign of Nebuchadnezzar Nebuchadnezzar dreamed dreams, wherewith his spirit was troubled, and his sleep brake from him.]

Daniel had a specialty in understanding dreams as suggested here: [Daniel 1:17 As for these four children, God gave them knowledge and skill in all learning and wisdom: and Daniel had understanding in all visions and dreams.] So this verse is saying Nebuchadnezzar was having trouble sleeping [his sleep brake from him.] because of the dreams so Nebuchadnezzar has insomnia and insomnia is a symptom of one that is nervous or anxious and anxiety is a symptom of the "curse" so this goes back to Genesis and is showing that these comments are happening [Genesis 3:14 And the LORD God said unto the serpent, Because thou hast done this, thou art cursed] and a symptom of that curse is [Genesis 3:16 Unto the woman he said, I will greatly multiply thy sorrow and thy conception; in sorrow thou shalt bring forth children; and thy desire shall be to thy husband, and he shall rule over thee.] = sorrow will rule over you, a symptom of the curse; and one of these sorrows is insomnia relative to anxiety or nervousness and thus timidity.

[Daniel 2:2 Then the king commanded to call the magicians, and the astrologers, and the sorcerers, and the Chaldeans, for to shew the king his dreams. So they came and stood before the king.]

Nebuchadnezzar calls all of his "experts" to see if they can assist him with his sorrow, which is insomnia. One way to look at it is a blind man is asking his blind experts to assist him to treat symptoms of the curse.

[Daniel 2:3 And the king said unto them, I have dreamed a dream, and my spirit was troubled to know the dream.]

This dream is troubling Nebuchadnezzar and this is causing him insomnia so he seeks these experts to explain it to him to relieve his suffering.

[Daniel 2:4 Then spake the Chaldeans to the king in Syriack, O king, live for ever: tell thy servants the dream, and we will shew the interpretation.]

Syriack is a language classified as Middle Aramaic so the Chaldeans were speaking a foreign tongue which suggests they were scribes because they knew this Syriack written language. So this is suggesting the written language "brand" is not relevant because all written languages are the same thing relative to they are linear left brain based inventions and in order to learn any written language one has to favor left hemisphere. This is a very subtle comment because Daniel made sure to mention these Chaldeans were a different kind of scribe meaning they used a different written language. This is relative to the comment in Genesis : [Genesis

256

11:1 And the whole earth was of one language, and of one speech.] This one language was right brain non verbal communication, telepathy in part. So the written language veiled right hemisphere and then humans were only left with left brain verbal communication and then these divisions called countries and kingdoms came about and with that came many versions of the written language. This is complex perhaps because it does not mean left brain verbal communication was not happening because of written language it just means there was this non verbal and verbal communication happening, spoken communication and non verbal communication was the one language. Another way to look at it is, if you knew every time you spoke the person you spoke to could read your mind and tell exactly what you were up to, you would be think twice about attempting to deceive them with your words. So the Chaldeans asked Nebuchadnezzar to tell them his dream and they assured Nebuchadnezzar they would tell him what it meant so the Nebuchadnezzar could sleep.

[Daniel 2:5 The king answered and said to the Chaldeans, The thing is gone from me: if ye will not make known unto me the dream, with the interpretation thereof, ye shall be cut in pieces, and your houses shall be made a dunghill.]

Nebuchadnezzar then informs his "expert" scribes he does not recall the dream and if they do not remind him what it was and interpret the dream he would kill them.

[Daniel 2:6 But if ye shew the dream, and the interpretation thereof, ye shall receive of me gifts and rewards and great honour: therefore shew me the dream, and the interpretation thereof.]

This is just a repeat of the above verse. It is saying not only do you have to interpret the dream I am not going to even tell you what the dream was and if you do you will get rewarded and if you do not you will get killed.

[Daniel 2:7 They answered again and said, Let the king tell his servants the dream, and we will shew the interpretation of it.]

This verse is saying the experts were asking Nebuchadnezzar to at least tell them the dream so they can interpret it so this demonstrates the "expert" scribes did not have the right brain intuition aspect therefore they could not figure out what the dream was.

[Daniel 2:8 The king answered and said, I know of certainty that ye would gain the time, because ye see the thing is gone from me.]

Nebuchadnezzar is telling his experts he does not recall the dream, he is saying I forgot the dream. This may be Nebuchadnezzar testing his experts to see if they really are experts. It would be along the lines of putting them to the test and would be similar to today when some psychic is put to the test in a real way and shown to be a false psychic, so to speak.

[Daniel 2:9 But if ye will not make known unto me the dream, there is but one decree for you: for ye have prepared lying and corrupt words to speak before me, till the time be changed: therefore tell me the dream, and I shall know that ye can shew me the interpretation thereof.]

Nebuchadnezzar is saying if you cannot determine what the dream is you cannot determine what the dream means and that will prove you are lying about being "experts".

[Daniel 2:10 The Chaldeans answered before the king, and said, There is not a man upon the earth that can shew the king's matter: therefore there is no king, lord, nor ruler, that asked such things at any magician, or astrologer, or Chaldean.]

The Chaldeans are saying no being on the planet can determine what your dream is.

[Daniel 2:11 And it is a rare thing that the king requireth, and there is none other that can shew it before the king, except the gods, whose dwelling is not with flesh.]

The Chaldeans are saying it is rare for anyone to ask such a difficult task of them, to determine not only what the dream was but also determine what the meaning of the dream is. They are saying only a god could ever determine what the dream is. This is showing firstly the "experts" have no right brain intuition and also showing they are easily defeated bad also they don;' believe human beings have very powerful minds when they are sound minds or have the third mind aspect working so they have self esteem issues and that is logical because they are mentally hindered from learning the education technology.

[Daniel 2:12 For this cause the king was angry and very furious, and commanded to destroy all the wise men of Babylon.]

Nebuchadnezzar is very upset that he just found out all his "experts" were false or frauds and so he wanted them all to be killed. These beings [magicians, and the astrologers, and the sorcerers, and the Chaldeans(scribes)] are just like a person who says they can do supernatural things like pray and heal you, or like pray and make everything better and then you give them an offering or money. They are false. Right brain intuition is perhaps not supernatural and it just so happens these "experts" did not have it at full power because they were scribes and did not apply the remedy and so they were just confidence men and Nebuchadnezzar tested them and found out they were just frauds and decided to kill them.

[Daniel 2:13 And the decree went forth that the wise men should be slain; and they sought Daniel and his fellows to be slain.]

So Nebuchadnezzar determined Daniel and the others arks held captive were like the magicians, and the astrologers, and the sorcerers, and the Chaldeans scribes and decided to kill them also. Nebuchadnezzar was unable to tell the frauds from the real deal, the arks.

[Daniel 2:14 Then Daniel answered with counsel and wisdom to Arioch the captain of the king's guard, which was gone forth to slay the wise men of Babylon:]

So Daniel spoke to the "sheriff" so to speak to figure out why Nebuchadnezzar wanted them dead, the arks, as well as the "experts". It is a bit of humor because it is saying in spirit, "Oh no the mentally hindered scribes have determined something and the determination is probably lacking cognitive clarity and reason and common sense so it is time for beings with cognitive ability, the arks, to attempt to talk the lunatics down from their ill conceived determination."

5/29/10 4:19 PM-

[Daniel 2:15 He answered and said to Arioch the king's captain, Why is the decree so hasty from the king? Then Arioch made the thing known to Daniel.]

[Why is the decree so hasty from the king?] This comment is suggesting the ruler scribe Nebuchadnezzar is impatient and patience is relative to time or sense of time. This comment is perhaps where the comment "Haste makes waste" comes from. There is no patience in the no sense of time perception dimension so one can appear to be quick to a being that is in the sense of time perception dimension, but relative to a person in the now dimension their don't perceive quick or sloth or slow or fast or patience or impatience because those concepts are time relative. These trends are of course probabilities.

[Daniel 2:16 Then Daniel went in, and desired of the king that he would give him time, and that he would shew the king the interpretation.]

So Daniel spoke to Nebuchadnezzar and told Nebuchadnezzar if he was given a bit of time he would do what the magicians, astrologers, sorcerers, and the Chaldeans could not do which is determine what the dream was and interpret the dream. So one underlying aspect that is being setup here is the kings "expert" scribes said this cerebral test the king is making, determine what his dream was, was acknowledged by the kings "experts" to be something only a god could do = [There is not a man upon the earth that can shew the king's matter: therefore there is no king, lord, nor ruler, that asked such things at any magician, or astrologer, or Chaldean.] + [and there is none other that can shew it before the king, except the gods, whose dwelling is not with flesh.] and then Daniel says "I can do it." The concept in this second chapter is along the lines of, in a storm do not panic. This king makes this impossible demand and the king's advisors are already defeated and saying "Only a god could do what you ask" but Daniel does not panic in the face of perceived impossibility and this is relative to his mind set. Right brain looks at impossibility as a challenge or another way to look at it is right brain is a poor judge or is not prejudice so all problems are problems and no problem is greater than any other problem or challenge so in one way there are no problems juts challenges, mental daily bread. Think about the mind set of a person that loses their job, their house and all their money and friends, like the story of Job, one with right brain veiled may panic and give up but one that has applied the remedy does not see that situation as anything but a challenge. This is not suggesting impossibility is not impossibility but one with the full spectrum of their mind to their disposal does not panic as easily as one that is lacking the full spectrum of their mind. When the mind perceives impossible challenges as daily bread then one never goes hungry.

[Daniel 2:17 Then Daniel went to his house, and made the thing known to Hananiah, Mishael, and Azariah, his companions:]

This is saying Daniel went back to the other Arks and explained to them the situation. This King is lumping all these alleged "wise men" into one group but these four arks are not like the other wise men they are arks which means they are skillful in all wisdom, they are sound minded. So this is reflecting on this Ruler scribe, King and showing he is making improper determinations. It is showing this ruler scribe is confused. In this comment [Daniel 1:20 And in all matters of wisdom and understanding, that the king enquired of them, he found them ten times better than all the magicians and astrologers that were in all his realm.] The King knows these four arks are wiser than all of his advisors but now he is doubting that and that is a symptom of confusion and confusion is a relative to suffering and suffering is associated which the curse caused by the tree of knowledge because one is lacking in their mental spectrum namely right brain aspects. The deeper reality is these arks are not wiser than other arks they are just wiser than the mentally hindered scribes and an ark is simply a person that applies the remedy the full measure and restores the third mind or Holy Spirit aspect.

[Daniel 2:18 That they would desire mercies of the God of heaven concerning this secret; that Daniel and his fellows should not perish with the rest of the wise men of Babylon.]

[That they would desire mercies of the God of heaven concerning this secret;] This is just saying they were concentrating on the task at hand which is to determine what the Kings dream was. They were using the god image in man right hemisphere traits or the third mind aspect, Holy Spirit, to figure out what the dream was and that trait is intuition. Simply put they were just using their sound mind to solve a problem that was on their plate. It is understood one right brain aspect is intuition but the power of that intuition in the third mind state is what is not clarified because it is so powerful and deals with non verbal aspects and its power is hard to explain in words unless one uses the

word un-nameable in power. So Daniel and the other Ark's are in a do or die situation, a storm.
[that Daniel and his fellows should not perish with the rest of the wise men of Babylon.]

[Daniel 2:19 Then was the secret revealed unto Daniel in a night vision. Then Daniel blessed the God of heaven.]

This is saying after concentrating Daniel figured out what the dream was and he blessed God in Heaven, right hemisphere, the god image in man, the third mind aspect.
For example: One gets the education technology and their right hemisphere is veiled, so then they apply the remedy the full measure and not only do they restore right hemisphere traits, they restore the third mind aspect which is achieved when the mind is unified or in the "middle" relative to the "middle way".

[revealed unto Daniel in a night vision] is just saying it came to Daniel by way of the intuition. Intuition is perhaps not magic or supernatural it is just an aspect of right hemisphere and is multiplied in power when in the third mind state just like all mental traits. If one wishes to go down supernatural street then modern society kills the god image in man in people with the verbal education and they do it by law and they do it by using "if then" statements like, get our education or then you get a slave job which translates as kill the god image in man in your mind or you get discriminated against.

[Daniel 2:20 Daniel answered and said, Blessed be the name of God for ever and ever: for wisdom and might are his:]

[for wisdom and might are his:] This is complex but to explain it simply, this third mind aspect one achieves after they apply the remedy to the full measure makes everything simple and one becomes a fountain of wisdom but relative to their perception they do not even have to try or wisdom comes easy. The education technology turns fountains of wisdom into mentally hindered retards and that is not an exaggeration and since the remedy is so harsh it is probable the education technology kills the being absolutely and deeper still it is not even understood if even after one applies the remedy how much is lost because of all those years of being mentally hindered.

[Daniel 2:21 And he changeth the times and the seasons: he removeth kings, and setteth up kings: he giveth wisdom unto the wise, and knowledge to them that know understanding:]

This is just Daniel attempting to explain how wise right hemisphere and thus this third mind aspect which is achieved when one applies the remedy. Daniel is trying to say this third mind aspect is so powerful I cannot explain it in words because it is a cerebral aspect and thus many aspects are non verbal and simply cannot be explained in words. "I once was blind (a scribe) but now I see (applied the remedy)." pretty much sums it up.

[Daniel 2:22 He revealeth the deep and secret things: he knoweth what is in the darkness, and the light dwelleth with him.]

[He revealeth the deep and secret things] This is speaking about several aspects of this third mind, one being of course intuition and also this pattern detection. The intuition allows one to know things without seeing them and the pattern detection allows one to look at large amounts of data and comb understandings out of them or as explained by Jesus in the Gospel of Thomas :

[He revealeth the deep and secret things] =[5 Jesus said, "Know what is in front of your face, and what is hidden from you will be disclosed to you. For there is nothing hidden that will not be revealed. [And there is nothing buried that will not be raised."]
Simply put with the power of this intuition and pattern detection magnified in this third mind state one can "see" or detect things they never could "see" or detect before they applied the remedy so after the remedy one may start suggesting things like "I once was blind but now I see" and then the scribes will conclude "Oh you are a religious nut." ; silly conclusions of the scribes.

[Daniel 2:23 I thank thee, and praise thee, O thou God of my fathers, who hast given me wisdom and might, and hast made known unto me now what we desired of thee: for thou hast now made known unto us the king's matter.]

This verse is Daniel explaining how he is pleased his three friends, the arks and himself will not be killed by a lunatic scribe ruler because they passed this impossible test the scribe ruler put them to.

[Daniel 2:24 Therefore Daniel went in unto Arioch, whom the king had ordained to destroy the wise men of Babylon: he went and said thus unto him; Destroy not the wise men of Babylon: bring me in before the king, and I will shew unto the king the interpretation.]

This is Daniel asking the scribe rulers minion the "sheriff" to take him to "his leader" the king because he figured out the dream and also the interpretation of the dream. Keep in mind the only reason these four arks are in this situation at all is because this scribe ruler attacked their tribe and took these four arks captive because they were skillful in all wisdom and the scribe king perceived he could gain benefit by enslaving the arks by making them do his bidding, like interpreting his dreams, like advisors. The deeper reality is this scribe king would not need these arks if he just applied the remedy himself and also he would not need anyone to interpret his dream because he would be able to himself and so this is suggesting all this suffering the scribes create with their "determinations". One example of this is the scribes determine pushing all that left brain favoring education on six year old children is a good decision when in reality it could not be a worse decision. It is more humane to kill the child than to mentally hinder them and then watch them

268

try to function in life. It is more humane to kill the horse than to watch it suffer with broken legs in the dirt. The tree of knowledge has created a choice we have to make as a species and the choice is death or life and for five thousand years we have been choosing death. One complexity perhaps is after one applies the remedy the writing and math are fine but the problem is the remedy demands an extreme amount of mental self control in the middle of a hurricane so to speak and a scribe who is timid is not likely to pull it off. The mental damage caused by the education technology is one level of the problem but applying the remedy the full measure keeping in mind one is very timid in that mentally damaged state is the harshest aspect of the problem.

Not that I ever get off topic but there is this story about what they call Cambodia's "jungle woman", and the story goes this female lived in the wild for a number of years and she was spotted so the scribes set out some food in a stake out and captured her. Civilization so to speak attempted to teach her their ways like their language and their customs and just today it was reported she ran away back into the forest and the ones who tried to "train her" said she did not learn any language and she disliked wearing clothes. They labeled this female a animal human which is quite odd because she is clearly a human animal but one can perhaps see how "civilization" perceives it is "saving" this girl but in reality they are just attempting to control her and when she resists being controlled so "civilization" labels her stupid or wild or not human. There is a very clear reason some that apply the remedy down through history leave society and became hermits. There is a very clear reason why some religions have monks that isolate their self totally from society. It is hard to focus in the herd so to speak but also it is hard to be surrounded by the ways of the scribes and also be free. One has to take on a mind set of isolation from the herd, society, in order to apply the remedy but it perhaps does not mean one should leave society although there are some indications observing the scribes suffering for long periods is harsh on the observer. One can apply the concept of this "jungle woman" to how the indigenous tribes were treated. The scribes encountered the tribes and then determined the tribes ways were all wrong and so they forced their ways on the tribes and when the tribes resisted they were harmed or discriminated against.

[Daniel 2:25 Then Arioch brought in Daniel before the king in haste, and said thus unto him, I have found a man of the captives of Judah, that will make known unto the king the interpretation.]

[of the captives] This comment suggests there was not a war as in two sides fighting over land or resources this capturing of the captives is suggesting the scribes were simply taking these tribes captive to capture their "arks" the very wise beings. This concept is a mirror image of what happened to the Africans at the hands of the scribes. There are only a handful of human beings on this planet who do not have written language, do not have a math system and do not have any contact with the scribes and they are taken advantage of and looked at like they are stupid and dumb because the scribes cannot imagine they are the last vestiges of sane human beings left. This remedy will restore your mind but it will not erase what happened to you. The very fact the scribes do not even think all that left brain favoring education harms the mind of a child proves they are not even in the ballpark of sane nor even have traces of cognitive ability. So we have a situation on the planet where over time these scribes kept putting this luxury and reward system attached to the education technology until everyone was compelled to get the education technology just to survive and that is why modern society is simply insane people. There is a remedy but it is harsh and modern society will create far more mentally hindered beings with the education technology than can ever apply the remedy. So Daniel was a slave to insane people and insane people make unreasonable requests yet because they are insane they continue to make more insane people so they have the majority and thus they have free reign to make everyone insane and that is what is happening and that is all that has been happening for 5400 years. There has never been any progress against the scribes as a whole because they cannot be reasoned with because they are insane. The scribes deeds and actions are perceived to be wise from their point of view but in reality their deeds and actions are insane and unreasonable and lacking wisdom.

[Daniel 2:26 The king answered and said to Daniel, whose name was Belteshazzar, Art thou able to make known unto me the dream which I have seen, and the interpretation thereof?]

[whose name was Belteshazzar] This is another aspect that plays out over and over. The Africans had names but when the scribes captured them slowly the Africans started adopting the scribe's names. The captives have to adapt to the captors. This is a very subtle form of control. So in Daniels case not only did the scribes take him captive along with the other three arks but also perhaps many beings of that particular tribe but they also forced their names on him. So Daniel is suggesting the name he was given by his captors but he is also denying that name and using his real name Daniel. Same concept happened to Native Americans also. The nature of this extreme left brain mind set is all controlling, it is simply anti-freedom on every level. It is not the being wants to be controlling it is simply left hemisphere has no intuition and also does not have very good foresight because it is linear based so it needs control or needs to be controlled to sense safety, yet this safety it seeks is relative to the timidity which is relative to the over active hypothalamus aspect. A scribe has the freedom to pass laws to put their self in a cage so they can perceive they are safe because they are so timid after all that left brain favoring education. To a scribe the word freedom is danger because freedom has too many unknowns and in that extreme left brain mind set one cannot see ahead but in linear aspects only. Because the scribes see only one step ahead their perception of the world is very scary. The scribes will pass laws that say "You cannot even do things that are only relative to you because it may somehow in this spooky world make me afraid." The amount of laws the scribes have is relative to their vast timidity caused by the education technology. Fear is relative to laws. Freedom is scary to a being that is timid. This Cambodia's "jungle woman" willingly walked out of a "safe" house that provided lots of food and lots of safety and went back into the "spooky scary" jungle. That appears crazy to a timid person and that appears logical to a being that is not timid. Death is no more likely in a jungle than it is in a house unless one is an emotional, timid, nervous wreck and deeper still in a jungle one relies on their own determinations but in society one is at the mercy of the herd. You are not living in a house because you are wise, you are living in a house because you can no longer function in the wild. After the education ones hunger is through the roof, ones emotional state is abnormal, they are timid and thus all these factors mean they cannot think clearly so in stressful situations they panic and emotionally implode. The test of this would be to find a being that still lives in the wild over the age of twenty five, when the frontal lobe develops, and has had no contact with the scribes or the written language or the math and somehow teach them to communicate readily with civilization and civilization would then have access to a fully sound minded human being. The catch is insanity perceives sanity is insane. Just living in society after one applies the remedy is a challenge because society demands a person take advantage of everything around them. The scribes perceive someone that does not take advantage is taking advantage and someone that makes lots of money, has lots of houses, has lots of cars and buys lots of products is productive. Everything is backwards. The Buddha boy lives in the jungle and once in a while he comes back to civilization and observes it for a moment and heads right back into the jungle after saying things like "There is so much suffering." The wilderness is where it is safe from the scribes. I do not detect the cities or the houses or the other technology is the problem it is simply the education taught how it taught and when it is taught and then the remedy not being suggested or beings not made aware of the educations potential mental side effects is the problem. One can never adopt a holistic perception after the education, they have to apply the remedy to undo the "seeing good and evil" parts perception and this achieves the holistic perception.

[Daniel 2:27 Daniel answered in the presence of the king, and said, The secret which the king hath demanded cannot the wise men, the astrologers, the magicians, the soothsayers, shew unto the king;]

This is Daniel saying I can do what all your wise advisors cannot do.

5/30/10 2:31 PM

[Daniel 2:28 But there is a God in heaven that revealeth secrets, and maketh known to the king Nebuchadnezzar what shall be in the latter days. Thy dream, and the visions of thy head upon thy bed, are these;]

[there is a God in heaven that revealeth secrets] = This third mind aspect has intuition and the intuition makes the unseen seen.[But there is a God in heaven] This comment is Daniel attempting to say "It is not me in particular but this God image, this third mind aspect, this right hemisphere."One of the main problems in communicating with the scribes is this cerebral world does not translate well to their materialistic world perceptions. Another way to look at it is there is no money in the cerebral world so the scribes cannot relate to it readily which means the numbers do not add up for the scribes.

[Daniel 2:29 As for thee, O king, thy thoughts came into thy mind upon thy bed, what should come to pass hereafter: and he that revealeth secrets maketh known to thee what shall come to pass.]

[O king, thy thoughts came into thy mind upon thy bed] = I read your mind using the intuition. Note the words "thoughts" and "mind" and so this "thing" Daniel is doing is known as telepathy which is intuition, right hemisphere non verbal communication.

[Daniel 2:30 But as for me, this secret is not revealed to me for any wisdom that I have more than any living, but for their sakes that shall make known the interpretation to the king, and that thou mightest know the thoughts of thy heart.]

[But as for me, this secret is not revealed to me for any wisdom that I have more than any living] This is a repeat of : [there is a God in heaven that revealeth secrets] which is saying "Its not me, anyone who achieves this state of mind can achieve these things."Now if one thinks about how the scribes perceive things they idolize all these wise beings in the ancient texts. They have places named after them and statues and have untold money making opportunities based on their names. These wise beings were always saying in untold number of ways "It is not me it is this God image in man that is the secret and the power and if you apply the remedy we suggest after getting the education you will restore that image, that third mind spirit and then you will understand it is not "me" it is "us"."

[and that thou mightest know the thoughts of thy heart.] This comment is simply Daniel saying he will explain to the King what his dreams mean and this is just like what a "psychologist" does, which is explains to a person the potential reasons for their thoughts and actions just in this case it's a dream. It's along the line of a person asking someone "Why do I do these things or have these thoughts?" So Daniel is attempting to explain what is on this Kings mind "subconsciously ", by explaining his dreams to him or the reason of his dreams. On the other hand Daniel is consorting with the enemy to save his life and so he is a traitor and one reason why he is not known as a prophet, of course there are not really any rules in this battle so I am certain it does not hurt Daniels feelings he is not labeled a prophet it is a "When in Rome" kind of thing. Jesus took the money of the scribes and threw it on the ground and told them to their face they were darkness and the scribes butchered him so he is known as a prophet and known to be unflinching when confronted with the sinister. There is a concept called "No mercy for the wicked." It is a paradox but essentially one will never convince the scribes of anything if they suggest the scribe's ways are anything but lacking reason. One does not reason with it, one commands it. Perhaps that's not going to go over well perhaps.

[Daniel 2:31 Thou, O king, sawest, and behold a great image. This great image, whose brightness was excellent, stood before thee; and the form thereof was terrible.
Daniel 2:32 This image's head was of fine gold, his breast and his arms of silver, his belly and his thighs of brass,
Daniel 2:33 His legs of iron, his feet part of iron and part of clay.
Daniel 2:34 Thou sawest till that a stone was cut out without hands, which smote the image upon his feet that were of iron and clay, and brake them to pieces.
Daniel 2:35 Then was the iron, the clay, the brass, the silver, and the gold, broken to pieces together, and became like the chaff of the summer threshingfloors; and the wind carried them away, that no place was found for them: and the stone that smote the image became a great mountain, and filled the whole earth.
Daniel 2:36 This is the dream; and we will tell the interpretation thereof before the king.]

The above is the dream the King had which Daniel interprets to save himself.

[Daniel 2:37 Thou, O king, art a king of kings: for the God of heaven hath given thee a kingdom, power, and strength, and glory.]

This is saying "The king is king not because of his own merits but because he was allowed to be King because of a higher authority."

[Daniel 2:38 And wheresoever the children of men dwell, the beasts of the field and the fowls of the heaven hath he given into thine hand, and hath made thee ruler over them all. Thou art this head of gold.]

This is just a repeat of the previous verse, it is saying something controls everything and is beyond the grasp of "men", the scribes, the beasts, the ones who are "fowl". "Children of men" is the offspring of the beast; "men" is scribes. So Daniel is insulting the King and the King has no clue that is what is happening. Strategic words; One can explain the remedy as, be mindful of death and when it arrives fear not or one can just say go mindfully lose your life and if suggested to a scribe that is too far gone it makes no difference. It's important not to get caught up in the details because the seekers will always seek and the chaff will always be blind.

[Daniel 2:39 And after thee shall arise another kingdom inferior to thee, and another third kingdom of brass, which shall bear rule over all the earth.]

This is saying: other kingdoms will come so don't think you are the end all be all. This is very similar to a concept where in ancient times a ruler had a messenger sit next to him after he won battles and the messenger would whisper in the conqueror ear as he was paraded in the victory parade something along the lines of "All victory or popularity is fleeting", which simply means, Nothing lasts forever so keep adapting or changing. Impermanence is permanent. The written language does not work when one is attempting to speak about complex paradox because one ends up inventing new words, but the words are absolutes so then one has to invent more new words, and then the words start contradicting each other and then a being sounds like they are confused but in reality it is just the written language only works in linear simple minded absolute ways and shows many flaws in the probable, possible and paradox aspects. Simply put the written language encourtages simple minded thinking and if one attempts complex thinking using the language they appear confused of appear to make many contradictions but that is really just the paradox aspect showing through and paradox is a symptom of complexity or probability.

[Daniel 2:40 And the fourth kingdom shall be strong as iron: forasmuch as iron breaketh in pieces and subdueth all things: and as iron that breaketh all these, shall it break in pieces and bruise.
Daniel 2:41 And whereas thou sawest the feet and toes, part of potters' clay, and part of iron, the kingdom shall be divided; but there shall be in it of the strength of

the iron, forasmuch as thou sawest the iron mixed with miry clay.
Daniel 2:42 And as the toes of the feet were part of iron, and part of clay, so the kingdom shall be partly strong, and partly broken.]

This is explaining the other kingdoms that shall come after the current "kingdom". There is a section in this comment that is very paradox related.
[so the kingdom shall be partly strong, and partly broken.] This is a symptom of complexity or paradox and suggests probabilities and avoids absolutes. So Daniel is saying this particular kingdom will be good bad or bad good. Something right in the absolute center of strong and weak. This is relative to the concept of "There are two sides to every coin."=paradox. It perhaps would not have gone over well if Daniel said "And then there will be a kingdom that will be medium strong or average." So the kingdom that is of iron is strong but also iron breaks easily so when the iron is mixed with clay which means can readily adapt or be open minded to change, clay is able to be shaped, it creates an aspect that is strong yet also changing because iron represents a rigid state. So if one mixes strength with adaptability a very durable aspect is achieved; partly strong and partly broken (bendable). This is a very accurate description of the eastern concept of the middle way. If one has too many rules they cannot adapt and if one has too few rules one is not very strong but wisdom is required to determine when to be rigid and when to be like clay. One has to be a proper judge to determine when rules should be ignored and when rules should be

applied but a strategy to always apply all rules all the time is the iron and that is a weak strategy. "No one is above the law" means "We will put people in jail if the break the law even if the situation was very complex and even if maybe they had a right to break that law in that complex situation." A being that suggests rules apply all the time no matter what will find their "iron" will crumble when complexity arrives.

There must be absolutes and also probabilities relative to absolutes, probably. One interesting thing perhaps about rules is the suggestion "Rules are made to be broken." This means rules in some respects may simply be fear conditioning aspects. One fear's what may happen if they break a rule so they are a slave to that rule and then one may find a certain freedom when they break that rule. The one study that showed when a person is in physical pain and then they say a cuss word that actually makes them feel better shows this freeing oneself aspect by breaking perceived rules. All that is happening is a scribe in pain says a cuss word they perceive is a rule not to say and when they break a rule they favor right hemisphere and the paradox aspect of right brain is favored so the pain they are in subsides for a short period. Sometimes a female having a baby will cuss to relive the pain. The complexity is if the female applied the remedy or never got eth education technology they would not be having much pain and so they would not need to cuss. So this is relative to this "curse" making people suffer because it makes things that should not hurt so bad with a sound mind hurt greatly in the unsound state of mind. Be mindful right hemisphere dislikes rules because it prefers to think for itself and left brain is the opposite so the absolute in somewhere in between those two aspects and it is very improbable a being is born and naturally has this rule about not saying cuss words hardwired into their brain because cuss words are relative to the time period and the culture. That's a nice way of saying no being is timid about saying cuss words they have just been told they should be timid about saying cuss words and many scribes do as they are told.

[Daniel 2:43 And whereas thou sawest iron mixed with miry clay, they shall mingle themselves with the seed of men: but they shall not cleave one to another, even as iron is not mixed with clay.]

This is perhaps very deep. The ones that are iron mixed with clay are the ones who apply the remedy they are in the middle relative to in "nothingness", one is a mimic just like a child, they are free spirits.

[iron mixed with miry clay, they shall mingle themselves with the seed of men:] = The ones who apply the remedy will be surrounded by men(the scribes) = [1 John 2:18 Little children, it is the last time: and as ye have heard that antichrist(scribes) shall come, even now are there many antichrists(scribes, humans that don't apply the remedy after getting the education technology, they didn't keep the covenant); whereby we know that it is the last time(sense of time is a symptom of the curse caused by the education).]

282

[even now are there many antichrists;] = [seed of men(scribes):] Seed denotes "ways".

[but they shall not cleave one to another, even as iron is not mixed with clay.] This is like saying "Blood is thicker than water " or "Oil and water do not mix." This is a perfect example of these two alternate perceptions not being able to mix. It goes something like this relative to this education aspect. I have been through the scenario so many times now it is like falling off of a log.

I say: Written education and math harms the mind of children because their frontal love relative to cognitive ability does not mature until they are twenty five.

Scribe says: So you are saying we need to not teach children education?

I say: No I am suggesting since the inventions harm the mind the children and parents must be warned and then they must be made aware of the remedy so they can restore their mind after they get the education.

Scribe says: What is the remedy?

I say: One has to get the hypothalamus to give them the strongest signal it can give, the perceived death signal and when it does just ignore it or pay no attention to it.

Scribe says: That is crazy and you are crazy and everything you say is crazy.

Sometimes they say nothing because they cannot connect the dots. There cognitive ability fails them. Sometimes they understand exactly what I suggest but that does not mean they will apply the remedy ah la parable of sower, the seekers always apply the remedy but there is little wheat and much chaff in this narrow. The full measure remedy a serious hardcore mental discipline exercise relative to a being that is timid so this disconnect or the inability to relate is apparent. Because the education makes one very timid and makes one ego and pride very strong a scribe will often assume it is personal. It is not personal, any human being that gets the education has to apply the remedy the full measure if they wish to get their mind back and since the education started when they were six they do not even know what a sound mind is like at all so they are being asked to seek something they never had. That is perhaps far too great of a burden. That is why this education conditioning taught to children with no suggestions of its potential side effects and no suggestion of the remedy after it is taught is a grave crime against humanity. Think of every single grave crime against humanity combined and this mental hindering caused by education is worse and that is an indication of how powerful this third mind aspect is and indicates what a great crime it is to turn it off or not allow it. Because the education alters ones perception on an absolute scale and in turn alters what that beings deeds are relative to how they interact with others and their self and the environment it is also a grave crime against the environment. If a person is given a mind altering drug and they in turn burn down the planet, the act of giving that person the drug is the core problem not the actual act of burning down the planet because that would just be an effect relationship to the cause of giving them the drug in the first place. We are not destroying each other and the planet because we are born with unsound minds, that would suggest a DNA shift in our species and that has not happened, so it is the education that takes our perfectly sound minds at birth and ruins it, and then the altered perception is what is making us act the way we do and perceive things the way we do. Here is a paradox. "I didn't know that."

[but they shall not cleave one to another, even as iron is not mixed with clay.] = [Luke 12:51 Suppose ye that I am come to give peace on earth? I tell you, Nay; but rather division:]
The scribe's versus the tribes is the division. The insane versus the sane is the division. The darkness versus the light is the division.
[Genesis 49:28 All these are the twelve (((tribes))) of Israel:]
Israel is not a place it is a being that has applied the remedy to the tree of knowledge. It is not a place relative to physical aspects it is the no sense of time perception dimension and relative to cerebral aspects only. Genesis 49:28 is simply saying "These are the human beings that have applied the remedy to the tree of knowledge to a degree and they are known as tribes because they are at division with the scribes who have

not applied the remedy. This division could not have possibly been around before 5400 years ago when Sumerian written language was invented. There is no country on this planet that even suggests there may be unwanted mental side effect problems relative to the education technology and thus no country on this planet that suggests the remedy to those mental side effects caused by the reading, writing, and math so they are all just scribes and nothing more than scribes, period.

[Numbers 31:4 Of every tribe a thousand, throughout all the tribes of Israel, shall ye send to the war.]

These tribes attempted to fight the scribes but the scribes were great in numbers and we well versed in war because they needed lots of weapons to protect them from their perceived fears and timidity. So the tribes did not have lots of war weapons because they were prone to harmony with their environment and the scribes had lots of war weapons because they were prone to disharmony with their environment.

This comment [Numbers 31:4 Of every tribe a thousand, throughout all the tribes of Israel, shall ye send to the war.] = [Luke 12:51 Suppose ye that I am come to give peace on earth? I tell you, Nay; but rather division:].
It is a very simple concept.
Harmony seeks harmony so harmony (peace) must apply self control to seek disharmony (war) to win this battle with the scribes.
Disharmony seeks disharmony (war) so it must apply self control to seek harmony (peace).

So the solution and the reason why this "war" has never been won is because the ones that apply the remedy are in harmony and seek peace and the scribes are in disharmony so they seek war. So to battle against the scribes is playing into their strength yet if one does not play into their strength they will unknowingly keep harming the children and making the children scribes or disharmony. Another way to look at it is the tribes are wise so they see this trap, having to play into the scribe's strength, physical war, so they seek to avoid that trap. It's the dammed if you do and dammed if you don't concept.

A person sees a crazy person with a gun held to a child's head, that child's is the fate of our species. If that person attacks that crazy person they may fire the gun and kill the child, if they do not the crazy person holds the species fate hostage. If that person attacks that crazy person they may get shot their self and also the child may also be shot. The complexity is that person is sound minded or in harmony and is not prone to do any of those actions but instead just let what is happening be. Letting what is happening "be" ensures the death of the species. The person in harmony also will see that as "is" so they will not seek to stop it because they tend to not be controlling.

So this comment [Luke 12:51 Suppose ye that I am come to give peace on earth? I tell you, Nay; but rather division:]is saying, you better wake up and forget about the holistic perception you are in after you apply the remedy because it is not reality it is just a perception of harmony the actual reality is we are killing our self off with this education technology by not questioning its mental side effects nor suggesting the remedy to its unwanted mental side effects nor warning people about its flaws.

Luke 12:51 is saying after you apply the remedy you better forget about your delusions of grandeur because we are in a pit as a species because of this education technology no matter how much your perception says we are not. One is never fighting for their self they are fighting for that child that is not born yet so that child does not have to get put in mental hell by the education or if they are put in mental hell at least give the child the benefit of the doubt and be sure the remedy is common knowledge to the species. When you mindfully kill yourself you might grasp that one.

[Daniel 2:44 And in the days of these kings shall the God of heaven set up a kingdom, which shall never be destroyed: and the kingdom shall not be left to other people, but it shall break in pieces and consume all these kingdoms, and it shall stand for ever.]

This comment is saying some day the tribes will convince the scribes of the dangers of the tree of knowledge and everything will be worked out because the remedy will be suggested become common knowledge in the collective of the species. This means one day the remedy will be understood and the dangers of the education technology will be understood and these kingdoms of the scribes, meaning the ways of the mentally hindered will go away. So Daniel had hope or faith.

"A causal stroll around the lunatic asylum shows faith proves nothing." – Friedrich Wilhelm Nietzsche

[Daniel 2:45 Forasmuch as thou sawest that the stone was cut out of the mountain without hands, and that it brake in pieces the iron, the brass, the clay, the silver, and the gold; the great God hath made known to the king what shall come to pass hereafter: and the dream is certain, and the interpretation thereof sure.]

This is Daniel playing on the Kings pride and ego. Daniel is saying "God certainly spoke to you in that dream and you are so wise God himself spoke to you and only you so you are fantastic and wise and a great king, now please don't kill me and the other arks you insane scribe beast." Daniel did whatever he had to do to save himself and that is why he is not a prophet. Jesus certainly could have played dumb when questioned by Herod and saved himself but instead he showed the chief priest scribe, Herod, nothing Herod could do could scare Jesus. This is a symptom of how difficult this situation is. Daniel was not less than Jesus it is just in a situation of probable impossibility one has to be willing to go any way the wind blows on one hand and also be rigid on the other hand. If Daniel would have told that King, "Yes your dream was from God and it means you are a jerk for taking me and my fellow arks hostage by force, and keeping us in cages."; it perhaps would have not gone over well and then Daniel would have been killed and then I would have one less book to translate properly in the ancient texts. "Live to fight another day" is a proper determination in some cases and "No quarter expected and no quarter given" is a proper determination in some cases. The deeper reality is no one convinced society there are dangers relative to the education technology so what they said and what they did worked on some levels but did not work on other levels. That's a nice way of saying if one underestimates the "curse" it is symptom the "curse" has already defeated them. It has never been about "Look at me" it is about "Look at what we are doing to our self with this education technology."

[Daniel 2:46 Then the king Nebuchadnezzar fell upon his face, and worshipped Daniel, and commanded that they should offer an oblation and sweet odours unto him.]

So Daniels play on Nebuchadnezzar's ego and pride worked and Daniel saved himself and the other three arks at least for now.

[Daniel 2:47 The king answered unto Daniel, and said, Of a truth it is, that your God is a God of gods, and a Lord of kings, and a revealer of secrets, seeing thou couldest reveal this secret.]

So now Nebuchadnezzar is a true believer at least up to the point at what Daniel suggested which was the King is a great king. Now if Daniel would have told the truth that King would have had Daniel's head on a plate in about zero seconds. It is perhaps interesting Daniel has not suggested the remedy to the King and that is perhaps to save himself. It is also possible Daniel does not know the remedy but that is a long shot. Of course Daniel is a captive and people behave differently when they are captive. People also behave differently when their life is in the hands of an insane scribe. Of course "insane scribe" is redundant.

[Daniel 2:48 Then the king made Daniel a great man, and gave him many great gifts, and made him ruler over the whole province of Babylon, and chief of the governors over all the wise men of Babylon.]

So this is where Daniel reasoned with the scribes and gave in to them. Perhaps this book of Daniel was included in the testimonies to warn one what not to do. This is very early in the text of Daniel so perhaps he comes to his senses but certainly this far in the text is showing that one cannot reason with the scribes because they may get the impression they are equals mentally speaking. Of course I doubt Daniel is concerned about this because he was perhaps employing the "Live to fight another day" strategy. Perhaps Daniel has something up his sleeve and he is breaking some rules in order to bring that plan to fruition. In chess sometimes one has to sacrifice some pieces to get the check mate. Anyone who applies the remedy will find the kingdom and the kingdom (Third mind aspect or Holy Spirit) is wise.

[Daniel 2:49 Then Daniel requested of the king, and he set Shadrach, Meshach, and Abednego, over the affairs of the province of Babylon: but Daniel sat in the gate of the king.]

So Daniel saved the other arks although they were not on the level of the big arks the "prophet arks" they were none the less skillful in all wisdom and the fact Daniel sweet talked this scribe king in order to save his life and his friends lives shows he was skillful indeed.

There is a concept called united we stand and divided we fall and that is relative to comment a house divided cannot stand. What that means is the education alters ones perception so they are in an alternate perception dimension and then there are some who apply the remedy and they return to normal perception dimension and these two sides will rarely see eye to eye on anything so that means our species remains divided. So if one group of the species is in one perception dimension(sense of time) and another group is in another perception dimension(no sense of time) cooperation is not probable so then we are a species divided against itself and it is probable we will not be able to stand. Anyone who applies the remedy will find the kingdom and the kingdom is wise. Education technology is not an effective tool since one becomes mentally hindered in the process of mastering it. - 5/30/10 - 4:45 PM